W9-DAC-649

MOBILES

MOBILES
BUILDING AND EXPERIMENTING WITH BALANCING TOYS

BERNIE ZUBROWSKI
ILLUSTRATED BY ROY DOTY

A BOSTON CHILDREN'S MUSEUM ACTIVITY BOOK

MORROW JUNIOR BOOKS • NEW YORK

Library of Congress Cataloging-in-Publication Data
Zubrowski, Bernie.
Mobiles : building and experimenting with balancing toys / by
Bernie Zubrowski ; illustrated by Roy Doty.
p. cm.—(A Boston Children's Museum activity book)
Summary: Constructions and experiments with different toys and
mobiles introduce the basic principles of balancing.
ISBN 0-688-10590-4 (library).
1. Mobiles (Sculpture)—Juvenile literature. 2. Balance—
Experiments—Juvenile literature. [1. Mobiles (Sculpture)
2. Balance—Experiments. 3. Experiments.] I. Doty, Roy,
ill. II. Title. III. Series. TT899.Z83 1993 731'.55—dc20 92-28408 CIP AC

Acknowledgments

Thanks to Arthur Zajonc, who checked the accuracy of the scientific content, and extra special thanks to Patti Quinn, who helped me put the final manuscript into clear and coherent form. Also to the fourth and fifth graders of the Farragut and Hennigan schools of Boston, who helped me try out the projects in this book.

CONTENTS

MOBILES

INTRODUCTION

Circus jugglers and acrobats are incredible to watch. These performers put themselves in difficult positions, balancing on narrow beams or high wires, or on the hands of another person. They may balance large objects in unusual positions for long periods of time.

Athletes and other kinds of performers are also impressive because of their agility and sense of balance. An ice skater moves at high speeds on a thin blade or spins on a narrow point without falling. A ballerina makes graceful turns and spins while standing on her toes. All of these people seem to defy the physical laws that govern our bodies.

However, they must all pay very careful attention to the basic principles of balance. Keen concentration and lots of practice have given certain performers great skill in applying these principles. Yet everyone—from an Olympic diving champion, to a small child learning to ride a bicycle, to you, reaching for a book on a high shelf—must master many balancing acts, great and small, every day.

The principles of balance are also very important in our living environment. Every house, office building, and bridge is a complicated arrangement of materials that are carefully balanced. To design a structure that can support itself, architects and engineers have to calculate the weight of the construction materials, and of the furniture or cars that will go inside or over the structure, and even the total weight of future occupants. Natural forces such as winds and earthquakes must also be considered in order to build a house or bridge that will not fall down.

As you do the activities in this book, you can be a scientist *and* an artist, just like engineer-sculptor Alexander Calder. He

is a well-known artist who made many toys and moving sculptures, called *mobiles,* in which balance was a key factor. You can gather simple materials found around your house (or classroom), as he did for some of his devices, and have fun creating your own balanced constructions.

By experimenting with toys and mobiles, you will learn about the very basic phenomenon of balancing. Getting objects to balance may seem quite simple at first, but as you work, you will discover that you must think carefully in order to really understand what is happening. As you construct and experiment with different toys and mobiles, you will begin to observe the basic principles of balancing. These principles can be applied to many other kinds of objects and constructions.

 NOTE: The cardboard you will need to make all of the devices in this book is corrugated—the kind found in most large boxes and cartons. And whenever you need nails, you can use finishing nails (the kind without heads).

BALANCING YOUR OWN BODY

Circus performers can do amazing balancing acts. You and your friends may have tried to duplicate them—and found that this type of balancing requires a great deal of skill and practice. The challenges in this section are much simpler to perform. They will help you think about how you balance your own body. All you need are curiosity, a few props, and plenty of energy.

You will need:
    4 books
    chair
    clock or watch
    pencil
    piece of paper

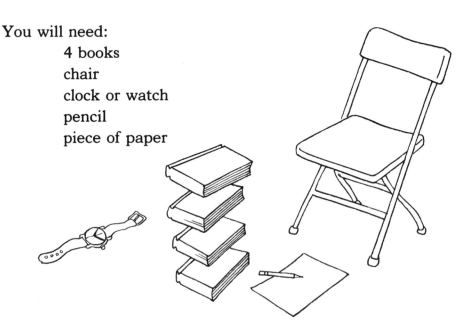

Challenges and Experiments to Try
These activities will be safer and more fun if you do them with a friend. He or she can time how long you can balance yourself in a particular position, as well as catch you if you fall!

- Time yourself to see how long you can stand on one foot.
- Balance yourself on one foot, raising the other foot a few inches from the ground. Then try standing with one foot several feet above the ground. Which is easier to do?

- Balance yourself on one foot while holding a few books in one hand. Next try holding a chair in one hand. Which is easier to do?

- Lying on the floor, support your body by the palms of your hands and your toes. How long can you balance yourself when holding your body a foot or two above the floor?

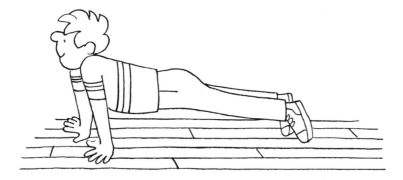

- With your arms extended straight, hold your body up, supported by two hands, then by one. Which is easier?

- Support your body with your feet and hands far apart.

- Now support your body with your hands and feet close together. Was this position or the last one easier?

- How long can your friend support your body when you lean backward while the other person supports your back with his or her hands?
- Try leaning backward against your friend's hands, tilting your body only slightly toward the floor (at a wide angle). Then lean backward with your body closer to the floor (at a narrow angle). In which position is it more difficult for your friend to support you?

BALANCING ON A BEAM

Circus performers sometimes balance on a beam. You can, too! You can make a balancing beam from a thick piece of wood.

You will need:
>   1 piece of wood, 1½ inches wide, 3½ inches thick, and approximately 4 feet long
>   2 pieces of wood, ¾ inch wide, 3½ inches thick, and approximately 2 feet long
>   6 nails, at least 2 inches long
>   hammer

Step 1. Center the shorter pieces of wood on either end of the long piece of wood.

Step 2. Nail the beam and the supports together very securely.

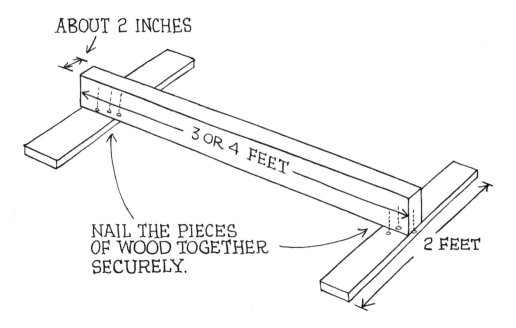

ABOUT 2 INCHES

3 OR 4 FEET

NAIL THE PIECES OF WOOD TOGETHER SECURELY.

2 FEET

Challenges and Experiments to Try

- How long can you balance your body on this beam?
- How long can you balance your body with only one foot on the beam?
- Is it easier to balance yourself when you are standing up straight or when you lower your body close to the beam?

- If you can find boards of different thicknesses, nail supports to them and make other balancing beams. Experiment to see which size beam allows you to balance the best.

What's Happening?

When you were balancing on the floor, you should have found that the more *points of contact*, or places where your body touched the floor, the easier it was to keep your balance. Two

17

feet on the floor is the usual way you keep your body supported upright. This position allows you to stand for hours. When you stand on one foot, it requires constant attention and very careful adjustment of your leg muscles so that you don't tip over.

Two hands and two feet give your body four points of contact. The entire weight of your body is spread over these four areas. When you remove one of these points by lifting a hand, you increase the weight each remaining point has to support and put your body out of balance.

Spreading your arms and legs apart makes you less likely to tip over when you try to support your whole body just above the floor. Likewise, when you balance yourself on the different-sized beams of wood, it becomes easier to stay in balance as you increase the thickness of the wood.

How close your body is to the floor makes a difference in how well you can balance yourself. Lifting your leg while balancing on one foot makes it more difficult to stay in balance. Crouching on the beam of wood, however, can help your balance.

When you lean your body on the hands of another person, he or she is giving you partial support. This support will increase as you lean farther backward or forward.

To help you understand what is happening in each of these situations, you have to visualize the relationship between your body and the floor. First, you must realize that the floor is pushing back against your feet or hands. Since the floor is hard and strong, it may not appear to be doing this. However, picture what happens when you walk through mud or hammer against a plaster wall. An indentation is made by the weight of your body or the force of the hammer. The mud and the wall yield because they are not rigid enough.

The more points of contact you have between your body and the floor, the more support you have, and the greater your stability. You are less likely to tip or be pushed over when you have four points of contact instead of two. It also makes a difference how far apart these points are. The farther away they are from one another, the more stable you are. For instance, it will be easier to tip you over when your two hands and two feet are close together than when they are spread several feet apart. But if you spread them too far apart, you would fall on your face.

When you lean your body against a wall while standing, the floor is no longer supporting your entire weight. Part of your weight is now being supported by the wall, and part of it is being supported by the floor. The smaller the angle your body makes with the floor, the more the wall is supporting you.

In the previous experiments, your friend takes the place of the wall. This is why it becomes harder for your friend to hold you up as you change your angle with the floor and lean your body more against him or her.

This last experiment will help you understand what happens when you try to balance your body or an object, such as the books or chair. If a body or object is kept perfectly upright, all of the weight is pushing down in one spot. If it is tilted slightly, this changes the direction in which the weight is pushing down. Some of the weight will cause the body or object to slip off the *balancing point,* the point on the object where it will remain in an upright position. (This is why it was harder to keep your balance while holding the chair in one hand instead of the books.) Unless a push is given in the opposite direction to counter this movement, you and the object will fall!

BALANCING A MODEL OF YOUR BODY

Circus performers can balance each other in very precarious positions. An acrobat holds his or her partner's outstretched body with one hand while the partner's arms and legs form various poses. If you watch carefully, you will notice that the supporting hand is usually near the center of the balancer's body. This seems to be the best place for supporting the human body. Is the center the only place, or does the balancing point vary, depending on the positions of the arms and legs? In this section, you will find out.

It would be difficult and unsafe to perform these circus acts yourself. However, you can build a model of your body and try balancing it the way acrobats balance their bodies. The model will not behave exactly like a human body, but it will help you discover how the balancing point of a body changes as the limbs are moved to different positions.

You will need:

> 2 pieces of cardboard, 10 inches wide and 20 inches long (This is the torso.)

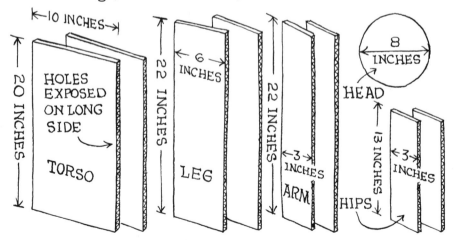

2 pieces of cardboard, 6 inches wide and 22 inches long (These are the legs.)

2 pieces of cardboard, 3 inches wide and 22 inches long (These are the arms.)

2 pieces of cardboard, 3 inches wide and 13 inches long (These are the hips.)

1 round piece of cardboard, 8 inches in diameter (This is the head.)

4 Fender washers, 1½ inches in diameter

4 regular washers, ⅜ inch in diameter

4 nuts

4 bolts, ¹⁰⁄₂₄ inch wide and at least 1½ inches long

1 piece of coat-hanger wire or any sturdy wire, approximately 12 inches long

scissors

screwdriver

masking tape

Preparing the Body Parts

Step 1. Using scissors, very carefully punch holes at two corners of each torso piece as shown. Punch a hole in the top center of each leg piece and each arm piece. Punch a hole near the center of each hip piece as shown.

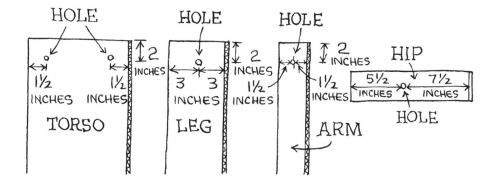

Step 2. Cut a 2-inch slot in each of the torso pieces and in the head piece as shown.

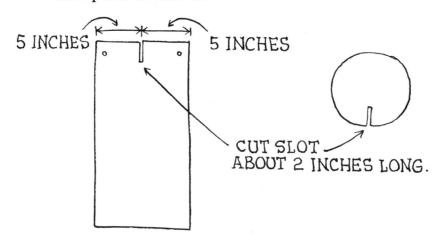

5 INCHES   5 INCHES

CUT SLOT
ABOUT 2 INCHES LONG.

Assembling the Body Parts

Step 1. Line up the holes and slots of the torso pieces and tape them together.

Step 2. Using scissors, score, or cut slightly on one side only, 3 lines partway into the hip pieces as shown. Be careful not to cut all the way through to the other side of the cardboard.

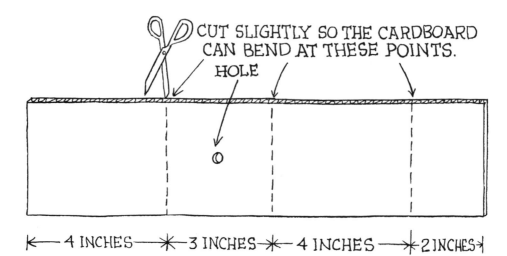

CUT SLIGHTLY SO THE CARDBOARD
CAN BEND AT THESE POINTS.
HOLE

4 INCHES — 3 INCHES — 4 INCHES — 2 INCHES

Step 3. Tape the hip pieces securely to the bottom of the torso. Each 4-inch end piece should be lined up on the back of the torso.

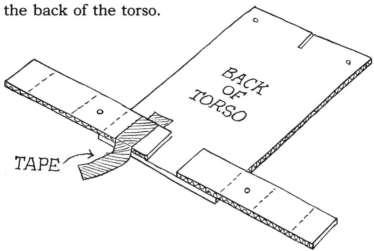

Step 4. Fold the hip pieces along the scored lines so that each 3-inch section is perpendicular to the torso and each 2-inch section lies flat against the torso. The remaining 4-inch sections will slant.

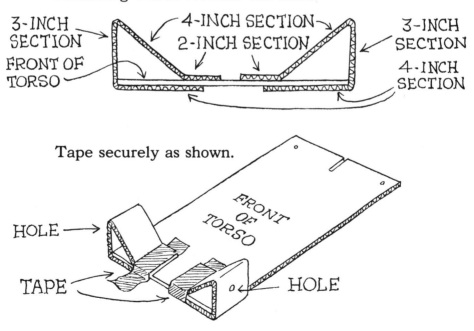

Step 5. Line up the hole in a hip piece with the hole in a leg
piece. Push a bolt with a ⅜-inch washer attached
through the holes and place another small washer on
the bolt. Place a nut on the bolt and screw it on.
Repeat this procedure for the other leg.

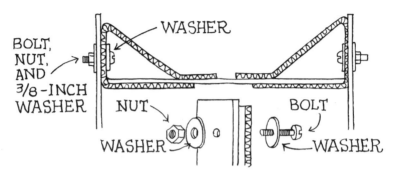

Step 6. Line up a hole at the top edge of the torso with the
hole in an arm piece. Push a bolt with a large Fender
washer attached through both holes. Place another
Fender washer on the bolt on the other side of the
arm, and screw a nut on the bolt. Repeat this
procedure for the other arm. Tighten each nut until
the arms do not swing freely.

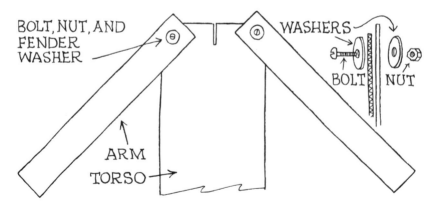

Step 7. Place the slot in the head piece into the slot of the torso
piece. Your model body is now ready to be balanced.

Challenges and Experiments to Try

You can balance your model of the human body in two ways: *vertically* (perpendicular to the ground) and *horizontally* (parallel to the ground).

Balancing the Model Vertically

- Use a fingertip on each side of the torso to support the model. Moving your fingertips up and down, find the point along the torso where the model stays just about vertical and doesn't tilt backward or forward. Have a friend make a pencil mark on the sides of the torso where your fingertips are. Label this position 1. This will show the point where the model balances.

USE ONLY ONE FINGERTIP ON EACH SIDE TO SUPPORT THE MODEL.

Ⓐ

- Try to balance the model vertically in the following positions.

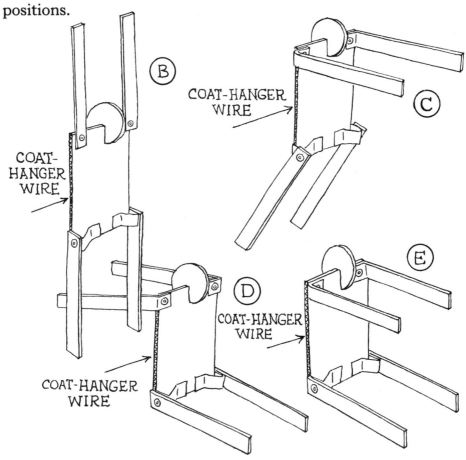

To do this, slide a piece of coat-hanger wire a few inches into one side of the torso, as shown. You will have to experiment with the position of the coat-hanger wire. Eventually, you will find the point along the torso where each of these different positions of the arms and legs balances vertically. Mark the position of the coat-hanger wire each time the torso balances. Use a different number for the balancing point of each position so you can tell each apart easily. (You may have to tape the arms and legs to keep them from moving.)

Balancing the Model Horizontally

Use your finger instead of the coat-hanger wire. Make a pencil mark where you must place your finger or fingers on the back of the torso in order to keep the model balanced.

- Find the balancing point when the model looks like this.

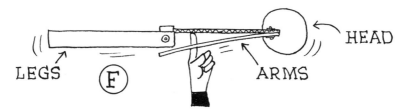

LEGS   (F)   ARMS   HEAD

- Find the balancing point when the arms and legs are in the positions shown. Make pencil marks to record your findings.

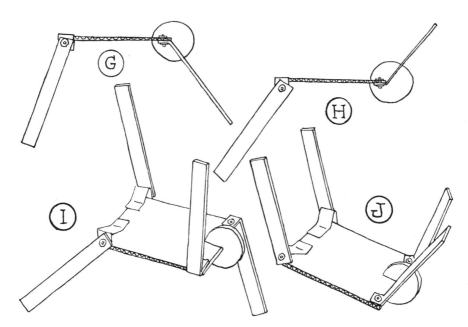

HINT: MODEL J IS VERY UNSTABLE. YOU'LL NEED 2 FINGERS TO BALANCE IT, BUT IT WILL STILL BE TRICKY.

- After you've tried these different positions, make up some of your own. (Remember to move the head, too.) Find the balancing point.

What's Happening?

As you experimented with the different positions, you should have found that the balancing points were close to each other for all the vertical and the horizontal positions. When you balance the model vertically as in position A, balancing point 1 is slightly above the midpoint of the torso. Did you notice that as you moved your fingers up from this point, the body remained vertical and did not tip easily? On the other hand, as you moved your fingers even slightly below this point, the model tilted very easily.

Balancing points 2, 3, and 4 in positions B, C, and D are slightly above balancing point 1 for position A, while balancing point 5 for position E is several inches below the others.

When you balance the model horizontally, all of the balancing points are close to the center of the torso, although for position F it is a little closer to the hips than for the others.

Did you find that position J required special effort because it was very difficult to balance? You needed more than one finger at the balancing point, and even then this position was still unstable, wasn't it?

The most important observation to make from this set of balancing experiments is that each different position of arms and legs changes the balancing point. The balancing point is usually near the middle (the trunk or torso) of the body. Changing the position of the arms does not change the balancing point as much as changing the position of the legs.

Changing the tilt of the head has very little effect at all on the balancing point.

These observations will make sense if you think about the relative weights of the different parts of your body. Your torso, including your neck, is the heaviest part of your body. Measurements of large numbers of people indicate that the torso is close to 50 percent, or approximately half, of the weight of the body. Your legs are about 34 percent, or approximately a third, of the weight of your body. Your arms are approximately 10 percent, or a tenth, of your body weight; and your head is even less—7 percent.

The weights of the cardboard body parts are approximately the same percentages as the parts of a real body. Therefore, the way your model balances is similar to a real body. Since your legs are heavier than your arms, changing the position of your legs, or your model's legs, results in a greater unbalance than changing the position of the arms. The head is even lighter than the arms, so changing its position has less effect on the balance of the human body or the model.

Remember, though, that the balancing point of your body is about the middle of your torso, rather than halfway up your body. (This depends somewhat on the length of your legs and the size of your torso, but this general rule applies to most people.) Later in this book, you will be balancing *symmetrical* objects where the center is also the balancing point. (*Symmetrical* means having the same size and shape of parts on each side of the balancing point.)

BALANCING OBJECTS

Circus performers balance objects of all shapes and sizes. It is fascinating to watch them work with large objects, because you can see how difficult it is to keep very big things in balance. However, even small, skinny objects can be very challenging.

FINDING THE VERTICAL AND HORIZONTAL BALANCING POINTS

You can experience for yourself the skill it takes to keep different objects balanced. Collect objects of different sizes and shapes from around your home or classroom. Choose some simple objects as well as some things that will probably present challenges. While trying to balance these objects or the models that follow, you can continue to learn about balancing.

Here are some objects you can start with.

several dowels, or skinny sticks, of different lengths,
for example:
1 dowel, approximately 3 feet long and ¼ inch in
diameter
1 dowel, approximately 3 feet long and ½ inch in
diameter
1 broomstick (without bristles), 3 or more feet long
several pieces of cardboard cut into various shapes
and sizes, for example:
1 piece of cardboard, 2 inches wide and 24 inches
long
1 piece of cardboard, 10 inches wide and 20 inches
long
1 round piece of cardboard, 8 inches in diameter
1 round piece of cardboard, 12 inches in diameter
1 triangular piece of cardboard, 10 inches on each side

6 or 7 drinking straws, joined together to make a long
piece

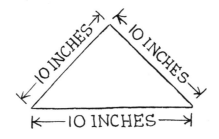

SQUEEZE THE END TO INSERT.

1 C-clamp (a large one will work better than a small one)

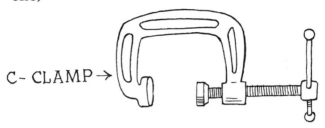

C- CLAMP →

1 piece of coat-hanger wire, or any sturdy wire, approximately 3 feet long, bent into a straight line
scissors
pencil
piece of paper

Challenges and Experiments to Try

 SAFETY NOTE: Do all your balancing outdoors or in a large space away from windows and other people. Keep all objects well away from your face.

- Try to balance each of the objects (except the scissors, the pencil, and the piece of paper) vertically on a finger. Then try using several fingers or your whole hand.

- Try to balance each of the objects (except the scissors, the pencil, and the piece of paper) horizontally on a finger or on your whole hand.
- Which objects are the easiest to balance? Which objects are the hardest to balance?
- Place a C-clamp on one end of the broomstick. Try balancing the broomstick, with the clamp at the end near your hand. Repeat for each dowel.

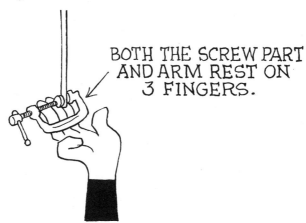

BOTH THE SCREW PART AND ARM REST ON 3 FINGERS.

- Does having the C-clamp in this position make it easier or harder to balance the broomstick and dowels?
- Try bending the coat-hanger wire into different shapes. Make a drawing indicating the balancing points for each shape.
- Make drawings of all of the objects you've balanced and indicate the balancing point. Keep these drawings for future reference.

What's Happening?

You should have discovered right away that it is easier to balance the different objects horizontally than vertically. The dowels, broomstick, and straws balance horizontally when you place your finger in the middle of each. Equal amounts of material extend on both sides of your finger. The pieces of cardboard also balance when you place your finger in the middle. The center of each circle is its balancing point. The triangular piece of cardboard balances once you find the point that is an equal distance from the three corners.

Even when these objects are balanced, they are still not very stable. If you push slightly on the far end of a balanced broomstick, it can fall to the floor. As soon as you push one end of any of these objects below the balancing point, the object will fall.

The coat-hanger wire balances like the broomstick and dowels when it is straight. However, it acts differently when it is bent. When you bend the coat-hanger wire downward at the midpoint, it becomes much more stable.

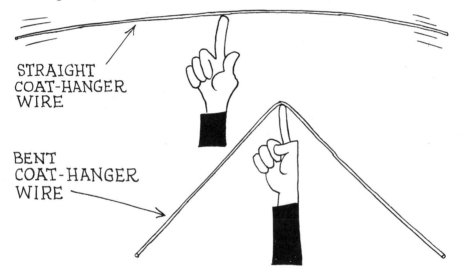

STRAIGHT
COAT-HANGER
WIRE

BENT
COAT-HANGER
WIRE

As you continue bending the wire into a variety of shapes, it will become more stable. Even if one end of the wire is bent near the top, it will not fall off your finger as long as most of the wire remains below the balancing point. Instead, the wire will swing back and forth and eventually come to rest in a balanced position.

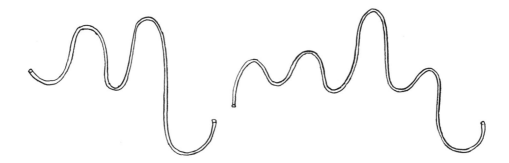

You can make a preliminary observation from this example. When most of the weight of certain objects is below their balancing point, they become more stable and easier to balance.

In contrast to horizontal balancing, when you try to balance these objects vertically, all of the weight of the object is directly above the balancing point. Each of these objects is very unstable when you balance it on your fingertip or even on several fingers. Unless you can keep the object very still and absolutely upright, it will keep tipping over.

If you can find a 1-inch diameter dowel, such as the kind used in clothes closets, you can make an interesting comparison. Cut the dowel to a length of 2 feet. One end of the dowel must be very flat.

Now try placing the flat end on a smooth table. If you are very careful, you can make the dowel stand upright. This is because the weight of the dowel is pushing straight down on the flat end resting on the table surface. If you jar the table even slightly, the bottom part of the dowel is disturbed. This, in turn, tips the top end away from a vertical position. This causes the dowel to start rotating about the resting point. Unless there is some force to make it return to the vertical position, the dowel will continue to rotate and will fall down.

Did you find that things like drinking straws and pieces of cardboard are easier to balance than heavier sticks such as the dowel or the broomstick? To help you understand this, imagine that the diameter and length of the straws and dowel were the same. The only difference would be their weight. A small section of the dowel would weigh much more than a section of a straw. When the top end of the dowel or the straw tips away from the vertical position, they will both start to fall. It will be much easier to restore the straw to the vertical position because it weighs much less. This action will be investigated further in the experiments in the next section.

By providing a wider base or adding some weight to the balancing point at the bottom of the dowel, you give it more stability. A wider base provides a greater resistance to the dowel's tendency to rotate at the base and tip over. Therefore, when you attach a C-clamp at the bottom end of a dowel, the dowel is much easier to balance. The clamp widens the base of support. It also gives stability to the vertical dowel by adding weight at the lower end. This counters the weight at the top.

The same thing happens with your body when you are playing sports. If you stand with your feet close together, it is easier for someone to knock you over than if you stand with them spread a few feet apart.

VERTICAL BALANCING

One of the most thrilling acts in the circus is the high-wire act. Far above the crowd, performers walk and change position while balancing on a slender line that wiggles and shakes. You have discovered that, even on the ground, it is not easy to keep your balance on a piece of wood several inches thick. So how do the circus performers manage?

Tightrope walkers have trained their bodies so well that they can remain vertical by only slightly changing their posture. Some also use long, heavy poles to help them stay in balance. This pole is usually held below the torso and kept horizontal.

Have you ever thought about why tightrope walkers use this pole? In what way does the pole help them keep their balance?

BALANCING A CARDBOARD SHAPE VERTICALLY ON A WIRE

You could try the following experiments using the model of the body from pages 20–24, but it is large and awkward. Instead, you can use a rectangular piece of cardboard to represent the human body. If you imagine a human body squeezed into a geometric shape, it would look somewhat like a rectangle.

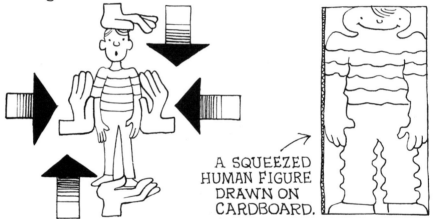

A SQUEEZED HUMAN FIGURE DRAWN ON CARDBOARD.

You will need:

>   1 piece of cardboard, 10 inches wide and 20 inches
>   long (This piece should be cut so that the holes
>   inside the cardboard are exposed on the long side.)
>   1 piece of coat-hanger wire or any sturdy wire,
>   approximately 12 inches long
>   1 pound of nails, 2 inches long
>   ruler
>   rubber band
>   1 paper clip, 2 inches long
>   pencil
>   piece of paper

Challenges and Experiments to Try

You can balance the cardboard vertically on the coat-hanger wire in a number of ways.

- Slide the coat-hanger wire through one of the holes in the cardboard and hold the free end of the wire. What happens to the cardboard?
- Do the same thing at several points along the cardboard. What happens to the cardboard at each point?
- At what point does the cardboard stay horizontal?
- At what point does the cardboard become almost vertical? Make a pencil mark there and call it the midpoint.
- Place the wire 1 inch below the midpoint. The cardboard will rotate so that more of the cardboard is below the wire than above it. To keep the cardboard vertical when the wire is placed below the midpoint, put the paper clip on the bottom end of the cardboard. Wrap a rubber band around several nails and attach them to the paper clip. Keep adding nails until the cardboard is just about vertical. How many nails does it take for the cardboard to reach this position?

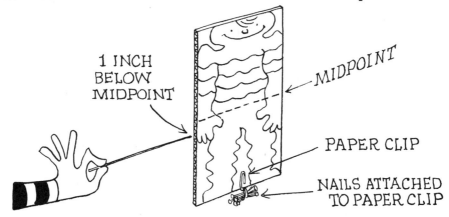

- Move the wire to positions that are 2 inches, 4 inches, and then 8 inches below the midpoint. How many nails are necessary to keep the cardboard just about vertical?

- Is it possible to keep the cardboard vertical when the wire is placed 1 inch from the bottom? How many nails does it take to do this?

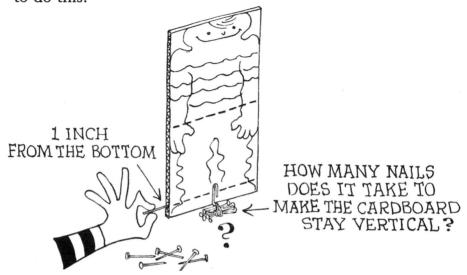

1 INCH FROM THE BOTTOM

HOW MANY NAILS DOES IT TAKE TO MAKE THE CARDBOARD STAY VERTICAL?

What's Happening?

The cardboard should balance horizontally when the wire is placed at the midpoint—the middle of the cardboard. The cardboard may tilt slightly on either side, but it does not rotate. As soon as you place the wire on either side of this midpoint, the cardboard rotates and comes to rest with the larger portion below the wire. You can get the cardboard to remain vertical by adding nails to the paper clip. When the wire is only 2 inches below the midpoint, you should need approximately 10 nails. As you lower the position of the wire from the midpoint, you need more and more nails to keep the cardboard vertical. (The number may vary, depending on the kind of nail you are using.)

The cardboard rotates when the wire is placed slightly below the midpoint because there is more cardboard above the wire than below. Even though it appears to be very light, the cardboard still has weight. When more weight is above the balancing point than below it, the cardboard will rotate. By adding nails below the wire, you compensate for the weight of the cardboard above the wire.

Placing nails on only one side of the cardboard may seem to run counter to your everyday experience with balancing. Usually weights are placed on both ends or sides of an object to get it to balance vertically or horizontally. Many balanced objects in everyday life have an equal volume, or area, on both sides of an imaginary midpoint. For example, your body has two arms and two legs, of the same size and on opposite sides, that you use to keep yourself in balance. Yet, as you have seen, you can balance a large area of cardboard with a small volume of nails. You will investigate why this is possible in later experiments.

Further Challenges
Cut several rectangular pieces of cardboard into different dimensions and carry out explorations similar to those in the last Challenges and Experiments to Try section. Make sure some of the rectangles have much longer lengths, or short lengths but greater widths.

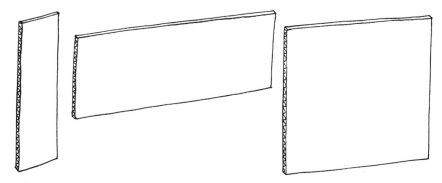

You can also create odd shapes and try to balance them vertically using the nails and coat-hanger wire.

A BALANCING TOY

There is a well-known toy shaped like a clown that can be balanced on a fingertip or a piece of string. This toy is fun to play with because even though it looks as if it is going to fall, it doesn't.

You can make a cardboard model similar to this toy and experiment with it to see how it works. The piece of cardboard from the previous activity can be used for the clown's body.

Your challenge is to make this cardboard toy balance on your finger vertically using only two other smaller pieces of cardboard and some nails.

You will need:

        1 piece of cardboard, 10 inches wide and 20 inches long

        2 pieces of cardboard, 2 inches wide and 24 inches long

        several nails, 2 inches long

        rubber bands

        several feet of thin string

        scissors

A Beginning Challenge

Before reading the next section, assemble the above materials and see if you can design an arrangement in which the larger piece of cardboard balances vertically on your finger. If you have a difficult time doing this, read on for some help.

Step 1. Score, or cut slightly on one side only, a line down the middle of the length of each of the smaller pieces of cardboard. Be careful not to cut through the cardboard.

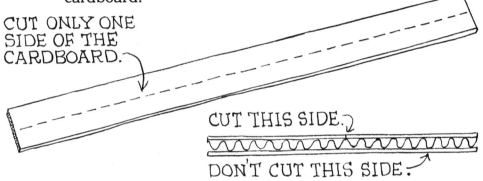

CUT ONLY ONE SIDE OF THE CARDBOARD.

CUT THIS SIDE.

DON'T CUT THIS SIDE.

Step 2. Make a slit 3 to 4 inches long in one end of each of the smaller pieces of cardboard. Bend the smaller pieces of cardboard along the scored side.

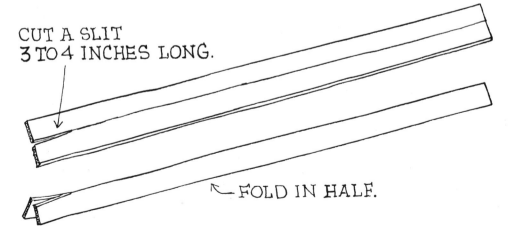

CUT A SLIT 3 TO 4 INCHES LONG.

FOLD IN HALF.

Step 3. Place each of the smaller pieces of cardboard along an end of the larger piece by sliding the cardboard into the slits as shown. Force 2 or 3 nails through the ends of each of the pieces to anchor them.

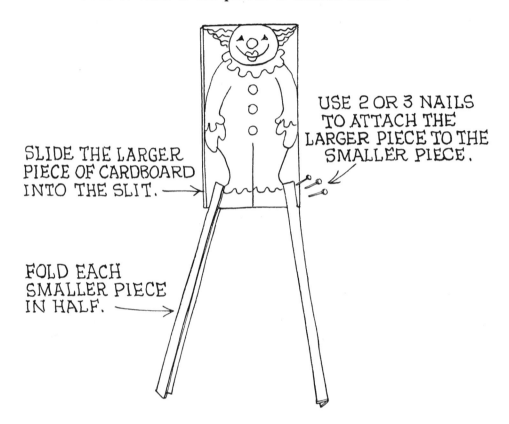

SLIDE THE LARGER PIECE OF CARDBOARD INTO THE SLIT. →

USE 2 OR 3 NAILS TO ATTACH THE LARGER PIECE TO THE SMALLER PIECE.

FOLD EACH SMALLER PIECE IN HALF. →

Challenges and Experiments to Try

• Place your finger at the bottom edge of the larger cardboard. What happens? Think about what happened in the last set of experiments. To keep the cardboard vertical, you hung nails below the balancing point. Try doing the same thing here. Wrap a rubber band around several nails and use rubber bands to attach a bunch of nails to each of the smaller pieces of cardboard.

- Try to balance the toy on one finger. (If the smaller pieces of cardboard are securely fastened to the larger piece and enough nails are attached to these extensions, it should work.)

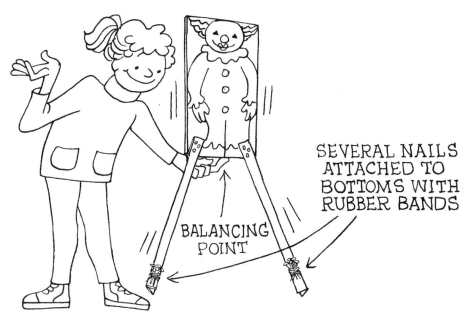

SEVERAL NAILS ATTACHED TO BOTTOMS WITH RUBBER BANDS

BALANCING POINT

- What is the minimum number of nails you need to make the cardboard balance on the tip of your finger when the smaller pieces of cardboard are hanging straight down?
- What difference does it make if the nails are placed at the very bottom of the pieces of cardboard? If they are moved toward the balancing point?

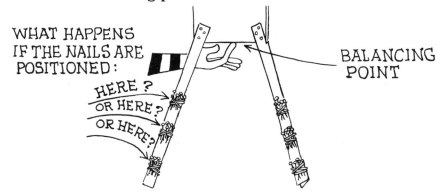

WHAT HAPPENS IF THE NAILS ARE POSITIONED:

HERE?
OR HERE?
OR HERE?

BALANCING POINT

- Can you adjust the number of nails or their position so that the cardboard is tilted at an angle but still balanced?

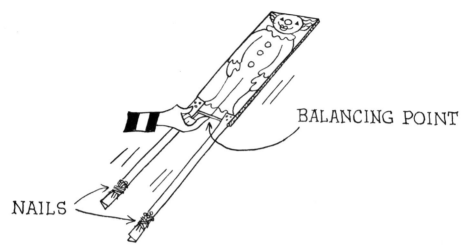

BALANCING POINT

NAILS

- Can you adjust the number or position of the nails to balance the cardboard horizontally?
- Can you still balance the larger piece of cardboard when a smaller piece of cardboard has been removed?
- Reposition the smaller pieces of cardboard so that they extend farther out from the balancing point. Can you still balance the larger piece by adding or subtracting nails?

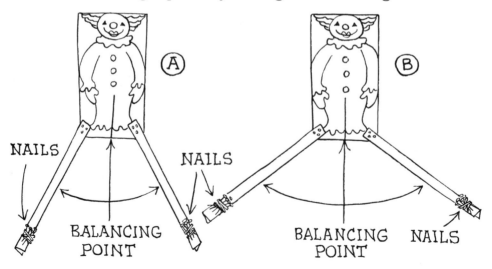

Ⓐ Ⓑ

NAILS   NAILS

BALANCING POINT   BALANCING POINT   NAILS

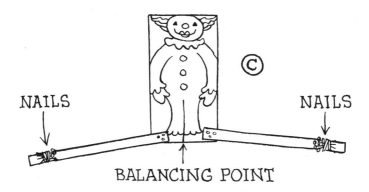

NAILS

NAILS

BALANCING POINT

● Can you balance the cardboard vertically on a piece of string?

What's Happening?

As you discovered in previous experiments, you can balance
the cardboard in a number of ways. Both the number of nails
and their position on the smaller pieces of cardboard are
important. The position or angle of the smaller pieces of
cardboard also affects the balance of your toy. When you
position the smaller pieces of cardboard just below the larger
piece, the minimum number of nails needed to balance the toy
is about 12 to 14. (This may vary a little depending on the
thickness of the cardboard.) Notice that this number is much
smaller than the number of nails you had needed to keep the
cardboard vertical in the previous set of experiments. Also, the
closer you move the nails to the balancing point, the more the
cardboard moves away from the vertical.

To get the cardboard to balance at an angle or horizontally,
you have to remove nails or move the nails closer to the
balancing point. And, as you move the smaller pieces of
cardboard farther away from the balancing point, as in
arrangements A, B, and C, it becomes more difficult to
balance the toy. In fact, arrangement C is very unstable and
nearly impossible to balance.

It is possible to balance the cardboard on a string, but it is a delicate process. You have to add many nails to the bottom ends of the two smaller pieces of cardboard, and the point where you place them has to be carefully determined.

These experiments suggest that not only the amount of weight but also where the weight is positioned in relation to the balancing point determines whether or not the cardboard can balance vertically. The farther the weight is from the balancing point, the less weight is needed to balance the cardboard. The closer you place the weight to the balancing point, the more weight you need to keep your toy vertical.

The results of your experiments have practical applications. For example, some sailboats have very tall masts and large sails. When the force of the wind pushes the boat forward, it also tends to tip the boat over.

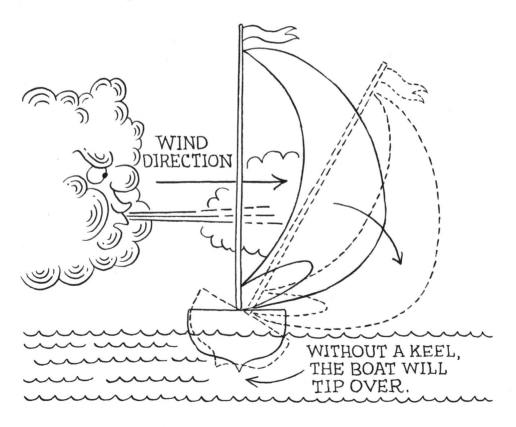

WIND DIRECTION

WITHOUT A KEEL, THE BOAT WILL TIP OVER.

To counteract this tipping force, a large, heavy extension is added along the center of the bottom of the boat. This extension is called a *keel*. The larger and taller the sails are, the larger and heavier the keel is. Often the keel is made of lead, which is a very heavy metal. The more weight that is added below the water-level balancing line, the more stable the boat will be—even in strong winds.

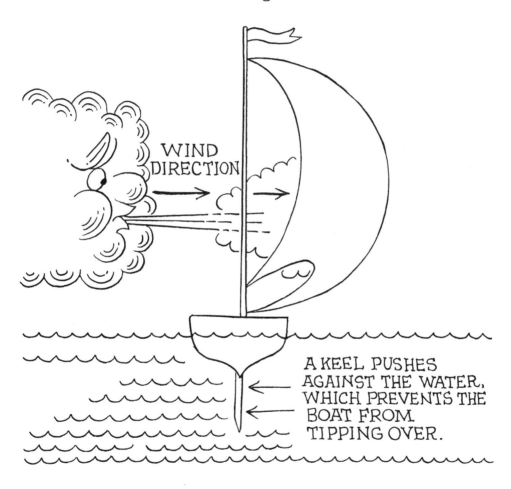

WIND DIRECTION

A KEEL PUSHES AGAINST THE WATER, WHICH PREVENTS THE BOAT FROM TIPPING OVER.

Boat designers take into consideration the strongest wind force that the boat might encounter, and make the keel heavy enough to counteract this force.

49

A ROLLING TOY

Have you ever seen a tightrope walker ride a bicycle across a wire? Sometimes this performer uses a long pole to help him keep his balance as he rides back and forth along a cable suspended high above the ground. This is quite a feat!

You can make a model of this tightrope walker to help you understand how this trick is performed.

You will need:
> cardboard balancing toy from pages 43–44
> 1 empty sewing machine bobbin

> several feet of ribbon, ¼ inch wide
> 1 pound of nails, 2 inches long
> rubber bands
> scissors

Step 1. Cut a small square at the bottom center of the cardboard. The hole should be the width of the bobbin.

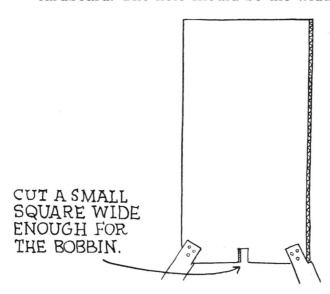

CUT A SMALL
SQUARE WIDE
ENOUGH FOR
THE BOBBIN.

Step 2. Attach the bobbin to the piece of cardboard by sliding a nail through the bobbin hole and into the cardboard as shown. Check to see that the bobbin turns freely.

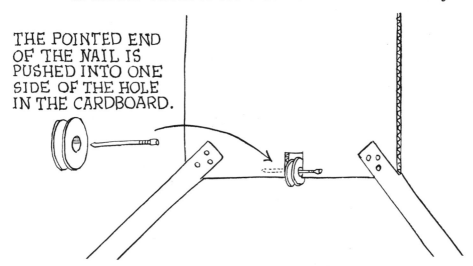

THE POINTED END
OF THE NAIL IS
PUSHED INTO ONE
SIDE OF THE HOLE
IN THE CARDBOARD.

Step 3. Use rubber bands to attach nails to the ends of the smaller pieces of cardboard.

Step 4. Add enough nails so that the toy will remain vertical when it is placed on the edge of a table.

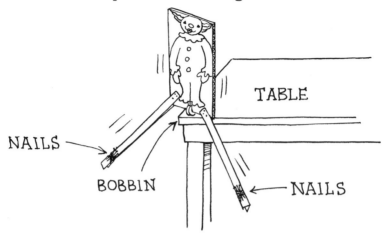

Operating the Rolling Toy

Hold a piece of ribbon horizontal while a friend positions the bobbin so that it can roll easily along it. You may need to add more nails to the ends of the smaller pieces of cardboard to keep the toy balanced and vertical.

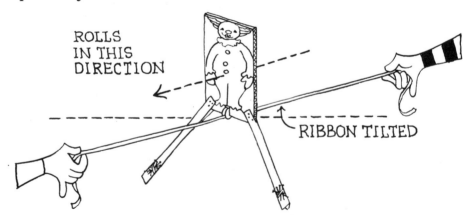

Tilt one end of the ribbon so that the cardboard moves slowly along it. By tilting the ribbon up and down, you can make the cardboard roll back and forth. This may require some practice, but eventually you should be able to make your toy roll back and forth smoothly.

BALANCING SYMMETRICAL OBJECTS VERTICALLY

There are many ways that objects can be balanced. In the experiments on pages 39–40, you balanced the piece of cardboard vertically by inserting a coat-hanger wire into its edge.

Another way to balance a piece of cardboard vertically is to insert a coat-hanger wire or nail perpendicular to its surface. An exciting real-life example of this is the circus act in which performers balance on a vertical beam.

This new arrangement makes it possible for the cardboard to rotate in different ways. The next set of experiments helps you discover some new properties of balanced objects.

You will need:

> 1 piece of cardboard, 10 inches wide and 20 inches long
> 1 square piece of cardboard, 10 inches on each side
> 1 round piece of cardboard, 8 inches in diameter
> 1 triangular piece of cardboard, 16 inches on each side
> 1 piece of cardboard, 20 inches wide and 40 inches long (optional)
> 1 nail, 2 inches long
> pencil
> ruler or straightedge
> pocket mirror

Challenges and Experiments to Try

- Can you keep each piece of cardboard balanced vertically when a nail that is perpendicular to its surface is punched through it anywhere?

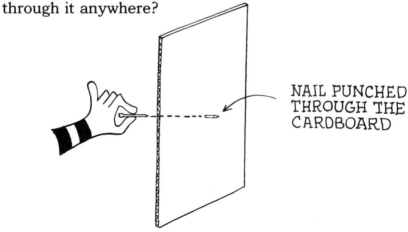

NAIL PUNCHED THROUGH THE CARDBOARD

- Making sure it is always perpendicular to the surface, punch the nail through each piece of cardboard at different spots. Mark the places on each shape where the cardboard remains balanced and does not rotate.
- Mark the places where the different-shaped cardboards rotate slightly when the nail is punched through.
- With the ruler, draw lines on the 4 pieces of cardboard as shown.

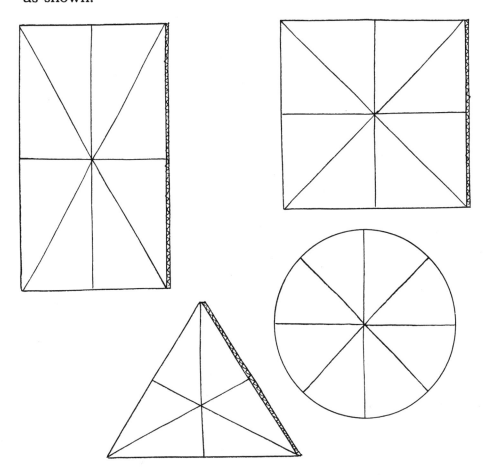

- Punch the nail into the cardboard at various spots along these lines. Watch where the cardboard rotates slightly and where it doesn't move at all.

What's Happening?

Did you discover that each piece of cardboard has one point where no movement at all occurs when the nail is pushed through there? This is the *center point* of the circle, the square, and the rectangle. The center point for the triangle is at the intersection of the 3 lines drawn from each corner to the center of the opposite side.

The vertical center line of the rectangle and the square, and the vertical diameter of the circle are special lines. If you place the nail at any point above the center along these lines, no movement occurs. If you place the nail anywhere along a vertical line above the center point of the triangle, the triangle will stay balanced. If you place the nail slightly below the center point along this line, each piece of cardboard will rotate until the center point is below the nail.

There are several important observations to think about in these explorations. You should have noticed that if you place the nail anywhere above the center point, whether it is on a line or not, the cardboard does not make a complete rotation. It may move slightly left or right, but it does not turn itself completely around. On the other hand, if you place the nail anywhere below the center point, the cardboard becomes unstable and rotates. More of the weight of the cardboard has to be below the position of the nail to prevent the cardboard from rotating.

When you push a nail through the cardboard on one of the lines, the cardboard rotates until this line is perpendicular to the floor. The cardboard rotates until it finds its most stable balancing point.

The lines you drew on the pieces of cardboard are called *lines of symmetry*. This means that there is an equal amount of cardboard on either side of each line.

To help you better understand the meaning of symmetry,

place a mirror along one of the lines on the rectangular piece of cardboard and look at the reflection. The area and shape of the cardboard in the mirror is the same as the area and shape of the cardboard behind the mirror.

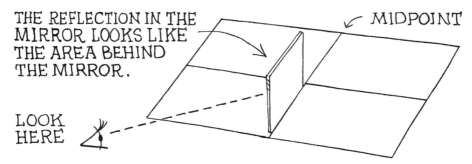

THE REFLECTION IN THE MIRROR LOOKS LIKE THE AREA BEHIND THE MIRROR.

MIDPOINT

LOOK HERE

The circle is very symmetrical. Put the mirror on any of the lines of the diameter, and the reflection will always give a complete circle. The square has four lines along which the mirror reflection looks the same as the area behind the mirror.

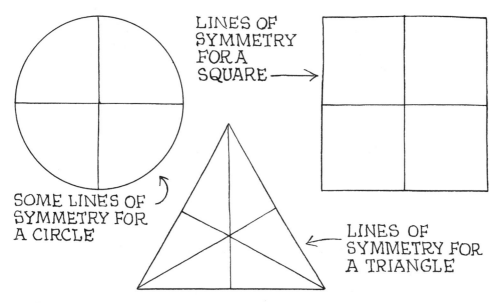

LINES OF SYMMETRY FOR A SQUARE ——>

SOME LINES OF SYMMETRY FOR A CIRCLE

LINES OF SYMMETRY FOR A TRIANGLE

The triangle has three lines of symmetry, and the rectangle has only two lines. The lines on the rectangle connect the midpoints of the long and short sides.

When you push a nail through the cardboard on any of these lines of symmetry, the cardboard moves until the line is vertical to the floor. The cardboard rotates until the intersection of all the lines is below the nail. Then the cardboard comes to rest.

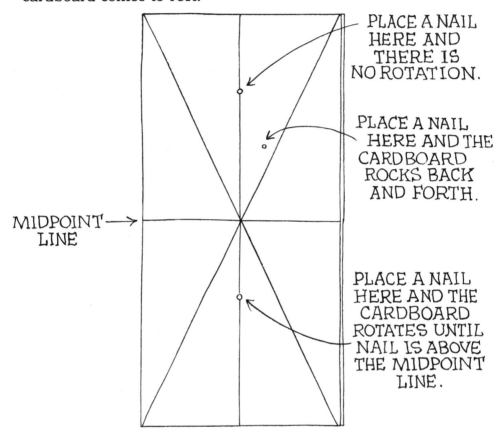

PLACE A NAIL HERE AND THERE IS NO ROTATION.

PLACE A NAIL HERE AND THE CARDBOARD ROCKS BACK AND FORTH.

MIDPOINT LINE

PLACE A NAIL HERE AND THE CARDBOARD ROTATES UNTIL NAIL IS ABOVE THE MIDPOINT LINE.

Each of the lines intersects at the point where the cardboard does not rotate at all. This point of intersection is a special one and is given a name by scientists. It is called the *center of gravity*.

All objects have a point where their weight is evenly distributed, or balanced. In symmetrical objects these are relatively easy to see and locate. With irregular objects they are less obvious, and finding them requires special procedures.

BALANCING HIDDEN WEIGHTS

In the previous set of experiments, each cardboard shape had the same amount of weight throughout the entire piece. Therefore, you could balance the pieces of cardboard in a symmetrical way at certain points. But what happens to the balancing point if the weight is distributed unevenly, so that different sections of an object weigh different amounts? You can find out here—and make a game of it!

You will need:
> the rectangular pieces of cardboard from page 54
> masking tape
> 20 to 30 nails, 2 inches long
> 1 piece of coat-hanger wire or any sturdy wire, approximately 12 inches long
> pencil

The Hidden-Weights Game

The Object of the Game
By adding nails to different sections of the cardboard shapes, the balancing points will change. The object of the game is for you and a friend to hide the nails in the cardboard and guess where they are.

Setting Up
While your friend is not looking, insert some nails into the edges of a piece of cardboard. Use a coat-hanger wire to push them farther into the cardboard. One or 2 nails will have little noticeable effect, so place at least 4 or 5 nails together in the same area. After taping all the edges to hide the nails from

view, write on the cardboard how many nails were inserted and in how many places.

Here are some places where you can put them.

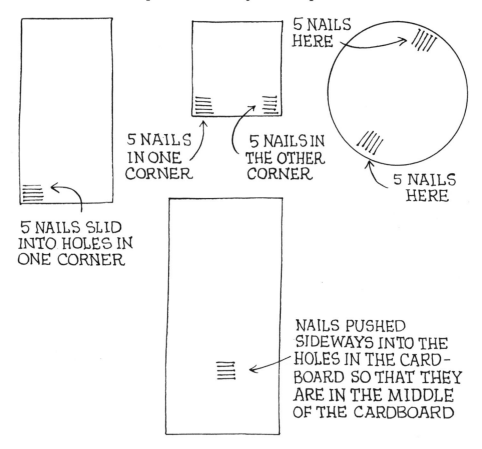

5 NAILS SLID INTO HOLES IN ONE CORNER

5 NAILS IN ONE CORNER

5 NAILS IN THE OTHER CORNER

5 NAILS HERE

5 NAILS HERE

NAILS PUSHED SIDEWAYS INTO THE HOLES IN THE CARD-BOARD SO THAT THEY ARE IN THE MIDDLE OF THE CARDBOARD

Playing the Game

After one of you has hidden the nails, the other person must try to figure out where they are located. The person trying to find the location of the nails is allowed to push a nail through the piece of cardboard at the midpoint and then at any other point. How the cardboard rotates will help him or her find the nails.

Take turns hiding and finding the nails using each of the cardboard shapes.

What's Happening?

You can quickly tell in which half of the cardboard the nails are located. The heaviest part of the cardboard will always rotate so that it is below the balancing point.

To find the location of the hidden nails more exactly, you have to insert a nail perpendicular to the surface of the cardboard at different points along one of the vertical lines pointing to the ground. The farther away from the center point you can place the nail without having the cardboard rotate, the greater the likelihood that the nails are farther away from the center point on the other side. The closer to the center point you can balance the cardboard, the closer the hidden nails are to the center point.

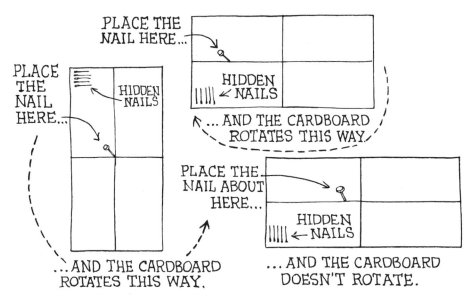

Locating the nails when they are not placed along the edge is more difficult. You can follow the same procedure as before, but now you must pay careful attention to the direction in which the cardboard tilts. The side that tilts downward will be the one with the nails. The more the cardboard tilts to the side, the closer the nails are to the edge of the cardboard.

To confirm your observations about where the nails may be located, tape several nails onto the cardboard on the opposite side of the balancing point from where you think the nails are hidden. Keep repositioning these nails until the cardboard rests vertically, without tilting right or left. Now you can conclude that the hidden nails are an equal distance from the center point on the opposite side of the cardboard.

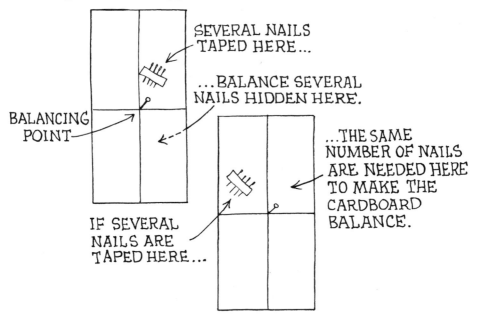

SEVERAL NAILS TAPED HERE...

...BALANCE SEVERAL NAILS HIDDEN HERE.

BALANCING POINT

...THE SAME NUMBER OF NAILS ARE NEEDED HERE TO MAKE THE CARDBOARD BALANCE.

IF SEVERAL NAILS ARE TAPED HERE...

Two of the pieces of cardboard have nails inserted in two locations. When you place the nail in the center of the circle, the cardboard will rotate until the sets of nails are in a horizontal plane and opposite each other. When you place the nail along the center line anywhere above the center, the cardboard will not rotate.

You may not be able to guess exactly where the hidden nails are located, but if you are careful, you can come close. The main observation you have learned from this game is that changing the weight of part of an object changes the way the entire object balances.

FINDING THE BALANCING POINTS OF UNSYMMETRICAL OBJECTS

The previous activity demonstrated that an unequal distribution of weight can change how an object will balance vertically. When weight was added to one part of a symmetrically shaped piece of cardboard, it was balanced by an equal amount of weight added at the same distance from the center point. What happens with an unsymmetrically shaped piece of cardboard?

In an odd-shaped object, different parts of the cardboard are of unequal weight and are at different distances from what would seem to be the center point. (In fact, such shapes do not seem to have a center point at all.) Can these shapes be balanced? Where would the balancing point be?

You will need:
>   5 or 6 pieces of cardboard, each at least 10 inches wide and approximately 20 inches long
>   scissors
>   1 piece of thin string, approximately 3 feet long
>   3 or 4 nails
>   pencil
>   straight pin

Step 1. Cut the pieces of cardboard into unsymmetrical shapes as shown.

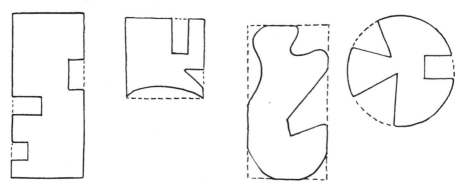

Step 2. Tie 1 or 2 nails to an end of the piece of string.

Setting Up

To locate the center point of an odd-shaped piece of cardboard:

Push the pin into the edge of one of the pieces of cardboard. Tie the free end of the string with the nails attached to the pin and let the string hang. Holding the pin, let the cardboard swing freely. When it stops swinging, have a friend hold the string against the cardboard while you draw a line on it along the path of the string.

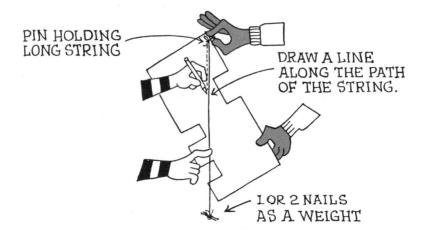

PIN HOLDING
LONG STRING

DRAW A LINE
ALONG THE PATH
OF THE STRING.

1 OR 2 NAILS
AS A WEIGHT

Now push the pin into another point on the edge of the cardboard, and let the string and cardboard hang freely. Draw another line on the cardboard following the path of the string. Do this one or two more times until several lines intersect.

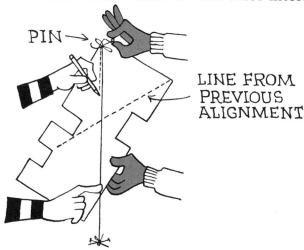

PIN →

LINE FROM
PREVIOUS
ALIGNMENT

Insert a nail at the point where the lines intersect. Hold the nail perpendicular to the surface of the cardboard and let the piece hang freely. If you have carefully drawn the paths of the string, the cardboard should not rotate. The point where the paths of the string intersect is the balancing point.

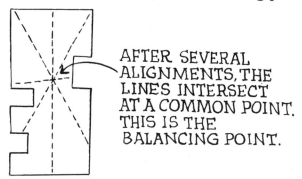

AFTER SEVERAL
ALIGNMENTS, THE
LINES INTERSECT
AT A COMMON POINT.
THIS IS THE
BALANCING POINT.

Challenges and Experiments to Try

- Follow the same procedure with the other pieces of odd-shaped cardboard. Always check to see if you have found the balancing point by inserting a nail at the intersection of the lines.

- Devise even odder shapes and try to find their balancing points.
- Before you attach the string to an odd-shaped piece of cardboard, guess where the balancing point is. Then test it.

What's Happening?

As you have discovered, objects have one point where they balance either vertically or horizontally. For symmetrical objects, this point lies on a line of symmetry. Unsymmetrical objects have vertical lines that function in the same way, but these lines are not as easy to determine as they are in shapes such as circles and rectangles. After you balance several odd-shaped objects, you will probably be able to make good guesses as to where the balancing point may be. But it will still be necessary to use the string procedure to find the exact location of the balancing point.

You have learned that the balancing point of an object depends upon the amount and distribution of weight on both sides of this point. With symmetrical objects, equal amounts of weight are on each side. With unsymmetrical objects, there are unequal amounts of weight on each side of the balancing point. A large amount of weight near the balancing point on one side can be balanced by a smaller amount of weight at a greater distance from the balancing point. This combination of the amount of weight and its location on the object determines where the center point, or center of gravity, will be found.

You can make another observation about the special point of balance of an unsymmetrical object. If you hold the piece of cardboard horizontally, you will find that the point where it balances horizontally is the same as the point where it balances vertically.

HORIZONTAL BALANCING

Acrobats in the circus balance objects and people horizontally as well as vertically. Performers in high-wire acts hang from the ends of bars while the person in the middle supports them. Still other circus acrobats climb on top of one another to form a human pyramid.

In each of these acts, all the performers have to be very careful where they stand and how they shift their weight. The slightest change in position could have serious consequences.

In one of the first activities of this book, you balanced a model of the human body horizontally and vertically. You saw that changing the position of the arms and legs shifted the balancing point of the model horizontally as well as vertically. Sometimes a small shift in the legs made a big change in the balancing point.

You will learn even more about balancing horizontally in this chapter. As you construct the toys and sculptures and do some new experiments, ask yourself if the same factors that determine how an object balances vertically apply to how it balances horizontally.

A TOY BALANCE BEAM

Some circus acts involve people balancing on a giant seesaw. Performers are stacked on top of one another or hang from a platform.

It wouldn't be safe for you and your friends to try this. Instead, you can build a model of a similar arrangement and then experiment with different stacking patterns to see how they affect the balancing of the main beam. Your own experience with seesaws will help you make predictions about what might happen.

You will need:

       1 piece of cardboard, 2 inches wide and 24 inches long
       2 pieces of cardboard, 2 inches wide and 12 inches long
       4 pieces of cardboard, 2 inches wide and 6 inches long
       8 pieces of cardboard, 2 inches wide and 3 inches long
       3 or 4 books
       1 coat-hanger wire or any sturdy wire, approximately 12 inches long
       2 small paper clips
       masking tape
       pencil

68

Step 1. The 24-inch piece of cardboard will be the main beam. Find the balancing point of this piece of cardboard by inserting one end of the coat-hanger wire near the middle of the long edge of the piece and repositioning it until the cardboard is horizontal. (You may have to move the wire several times.) Mark the balancing point with a pencil.

Step 2. Bend the paper clips partway open and tape them to the main beam at the balancing point as shown.

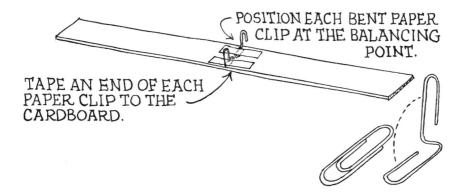

POSITION EACH BENT PAPER CLIP AT THE BALANCING POINT.

TAPE AN END OF EACH PAPER CLIP TO THE CARDBOARD.

Step 3. Slide an end of the coat-hanger wire into the middle of a stack of books. Slide the paper clips onto the wire so that the main beam hangs in a balanced horizontal position.

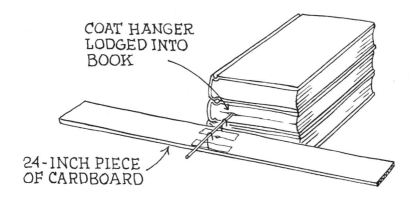

COAT HANGER LODGED INTO BOOK

24-INCH PIECE OF CARDBOARD

Step 4. Place the two 12-inch pieces of cardboard on either end of the device and reposition them until everything balances horizontally.

12-INCH PIECE OF CARDBOARD

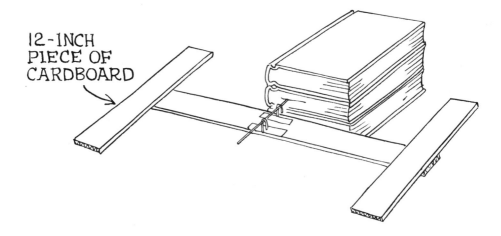

Step 5. Place one 6-inch piece of cardboard on each end of a 12-inch piece of cardboard as shown in the drawing. Reposition the pieces until everything balances horizontally.

6-INCH PIECE OF CARDBOARD

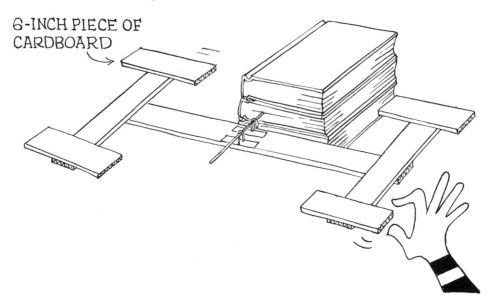

Step 6. Place one 3-inch piece of cardboard on each end of a 6-inch piece of cardboard. Reposition all of the pieces so that they remain horizontal.

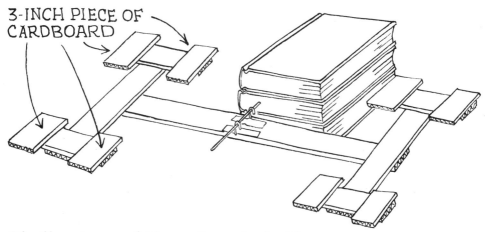

3-INCH PIECE OF CARDBOARD

Challenges and Experiments to Try

The setup you have constructed is a very delicate one. You will have to be very careful when you place the pieces of cardboard on one another so that they won't keep slipping off. Before you move the pieces on your balance beam, try to predict what will happen when you move each one.

- Move one 12-inch piece of cardboard toward the balancing point. Which parts become unbalanced?

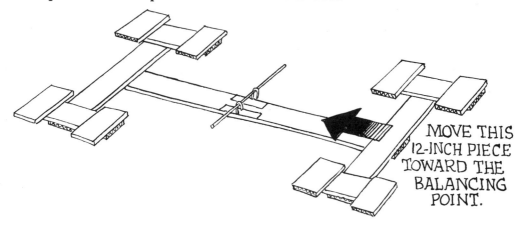

MOVE THIS 12-INCH PIECE TOWARD THE BALANCING POINT.

- Keeping both 12-inch pieces of cardboard in place, move a 6-inch piece of cardboard. Does the main beam change its balance? Does the 12-inch piece change its balance?
- Move two 6-inch pieces of cardboard so that they are in the middle of one of the 12-inch pieces. Does the main beam change its balance? Does the 12-inch piece change its balance?

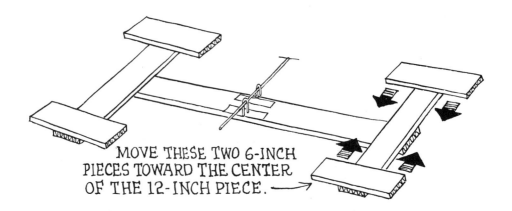

MOVE THESE TWO 6-INCH PIECES TOWARD THE CENTER OF THE 12-INCH PIECE. ⟶

- What happens as the same two 6-inch pieces of cardboard are moved farther out on the 12-inch piece?
- Change the angle at which a 12-inch piece of cardboard sits on the main beam. Does this affect the balance of the main beam?

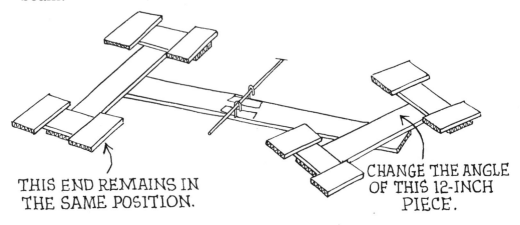

THIS END REMAINS IN THE SAME POSITION.

CHANGE THE ANGLE OF THIS 12-INCH PIECE.

- Move the 3-inch pieces toward the center of the 6-inch pieces. What happens to the balance of all the other pieces?

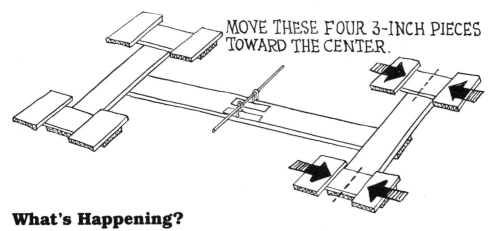

MOVE THESE FOUR 3-INCH PIECES TOWARD THE CENTER.

What's Happening?

In some ways, your toy balance beam acts like a seesaw. When you move an entire 12-inch piece of cardboard toward the center of the main beam, this end moves upward. The same thing happens when one person on a balanced seesaw moves toward the pivot point.

Rotating a 12-inch piece of cardboard at the end of the main beam can also affect the balance. When the 12-inch piece sits on each end of the main beam with half of it overhanging each side, the main beam will remain balanced. If you move more than half of the 12-inch piece over the edge of the main beam, this end moves downward. If the 12-inch piece is only partly rotated from the point where it originally balanced on the main beam, there is a very slight movement downward at this end of the beam.

When you place the four 6-inch pieces of cardboard on the two 12-inch pieces, the main beam will still balance, as long as you have not altered the original position of the 12-inch pieces. Rotating the 6-inch pieces doesn't affect the balance of the main beam. But moving the 6-inch pieces will affect the balance of the 12-inch pieces in the same way that moving the 12-inch pieces affects the main beam.

To understand this better, picture one board resting on your lap and another on your friend's lap as you sit on opposite ends of a balanced seesaw. Sitting two more people on the ends of each of these boards would still keep the seesaw in balance as long as the people were all similar in weight. Moving the people around in their positions won't affect the balance of the seesaw, but this movement could change the balance of the boards on your laps.

Taking this a step further, placing the 3-inch pieces on the 6-inch pieces will still keep the main beam in balance. Moving these new pieces affects only the balance of the 6-inch pieces. Moving the 3-inch pieces closer to or farther away from the middle of the 6-inch piece doesn't change the balance of the 6-inch piece. The 3-inch pieces already sit very close to the middle of the 6-inch pieces. The 6-inch pieces are too short to tip up and down on the 12-inch piece.

The overall observation to be made from these experiments is that moving the weight closer to or farther away from the point of balance will move the pieces from a horizontal position. If the beam is in balance and you change the distance or angle of the weight, it will become unbalanced. When weights are stacked on top of one another, moving the ones that are not in contact with the main beam does not affect its balance. This was also true for your explorations in balancing vertical objects. Recall what happened when you balanced the model of the human body and later made the piece of cardboard remain vertical. Once again, you have demonstrated that weight, distance, and angle are determining factors in keeping objects in balance.

A SYMMETRICAL MOBILE

The main beam and all the other pieces of the toy balance beam were situated above the balancing point. This is not a stable situation. A slight change in the position of the 12-inch pieces can cause the whole arrangement to tip.

What would happen if you turned this whole arrangement upside down? Imagine the smaller pieces hanging from the main beam instead of resting on it. This is very similar to a popular type of sculpture called a mobile.

One of the inventors of the mobile was a twentieth-century American sculptor named Alexander Calder. During his lifetime, he made hundreds of toys and balancing sculptures, including many mobiles. As a young man, he created a whole circus out of wire figures. His toys could perform some of the same acts he saw in the circus.

You can continue your exploration of balancing toys by making several different mobiles. They are not difficult to construct. Since all mobiles operate on the same general principles, they will help you understand how objects balance.

You will need:
>   the pieces of cardboard from page 68
>   thin string
>   1 package of thin rubber bands
>   5 to 10 nails, 2 inches long
>   scissors

Step 1. Place a rubber band around the middle of the 24-inch piece of cardboard. Wrap the rubber band so that it hugs the cardboard but is still loose enough to move. Tie a piece of string about 12 inches long to the rubber band. Move the rubber band to a place on the main beam where the piece of cardboard will balance horizontally. (The rubber band must be tight enough so that it will not slip when more weights are attached to it.) Tie the piece of string to a doorknob or to the edge of a table.

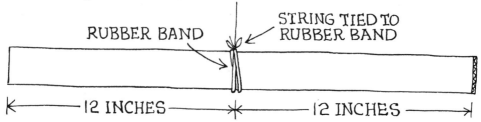

Step 2. Wrap a rubber band on each end of the main beam. Place the rubber bands as close to the edge as possible without letting them slip off. Tie a 2-inch piece of string to each of these bands.

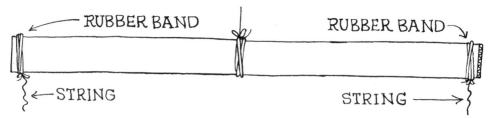

Step 3. Place rubber bands around the middle of each 12-inch piece of cardboard. Tie the loose end of the strings hanging from the ends of the main beam to the rubber band in the middle of each 12-inch piece. Next, place a rubber band on both ends of each 12-inch piece. Tie strings 2 inches long to the rubber bands at the ends of the 12-inch pieces.

76

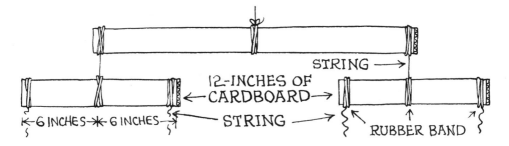

STRING →

12-INCHES OF ←CARDBOARD→

←6 INCHES→*←6 INCHES→ ←— STRING —→

RUBBER BAND

Adjust the pieces so that they hang horizontally.

Step 4. Place rubber bands around the middle and on the ends of each of the 6-inch pieces of cardboard. Tie 2-inch strings to the rubber bands on the ends of each of these 6-inch pieces. Attach a 6-inch piece to each end of a 12-inch piece. Adjust the pieces so that they are balanced horizontally.

Step 5. Repeat the same steps to attach the 3-inch pieces of cardboard to the 6-inch pieces. Balance the whole arrangement horizontally as shown.

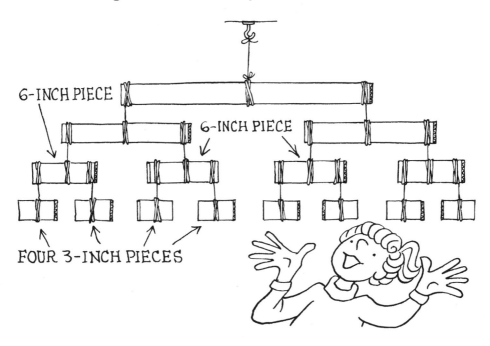

6-INCH PIECE

6-INCH PIECE

FOUR 3-INCH PIECES

Challenges and Experiments to Try

You can enjoy watching your mobile as wind currents or a gentle push make the different parts of it rotate. If all the pieces have been adjusted properly, they will move horizontally. You can also move the different parts of your mobile to make them tilt and lean at various angles.

- Move the rubber band on a 3-inch piece. This makes the 3-inch piece unbalanced, but does this unbalance the other pieces of the mobile? The entire mobile?
- Change the position of the middle rubber band on a 6-inch piece. Does this unbalance the 12- and 24-inch pieces?
- Change the position of the middle rubber band on a 12-inch piece. Does this unbalance the 24-inch piece or the pieces below it?
- Try moving the rubber bands on the ends of some pieces. What happens to each piece and those above and below it?
- Add a few nails to a piece at a time and observe how this changes the balance of that piece. What happens to the other pieces? The main beam?

What's Happening?

The mobile you made is symmetrical. There are an equal number of pieces on each side of the main beam, and the pieces on one side are the same size as those on the other. Since the pieces are equal in size and shape, the weight on one side of the main beam is equal to the weight on the other side.

In the previous experiments, you saw that as long as you didn't change the weight of any one part, an object would remain balanced. There would be a change in the balance, however, if the positions of some of the pieces were changed. This also happens in a curious way with the symmetrical mobile.

When you move the middle rubber band on any of the

pieces, you change the balance of that piece but not the others. But when you move the rubber bands on the ends of pieces, you can cause a major change. Moving the end rubber bands on the 6-inch pieces changes the balance of these pieces but not the ones above or below. Moving the end rubber bands on the 12-inch pieces, and especially the 24-inch piece, results in a big tilt. If you move one of the end rubber bands on one of these pieces, you can rebalance this same piece by moving the rubber band on the opposite end to the same position as the other one.

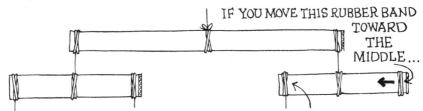

IF YOU MOVE THIS RUBBER BAND TOWARD THE MIDDLE...

...YOU WILL HAVE TO MOVE THIS RUBBER BAND TOWARD THE MIDDLE TO MAINTAIN THE BALANCE OF THE PIECE.

Compare these results to your results with the toy balance beam. Changing the angle of one of the 12-inch pieces changed the balance of the main beam, but changing the balance of one of the 12-inch pieces on the mobile doesn't affect the balance of the main beam. With the balance beam, when you move one of the 12-inch pieces, you change its position or distance from the balancing point. With the mobile, all of the pieces on each side hang below the main beam at one point. As long as this point is not moved, the main beam will remain balanced.

This happened with the toy balance beam, too. Moving the 3-inch pieces sitting on top of the 6-inch piece didn't change the balance of the main beam as long as the 12-inch piece remained in the same spot. This action will become clearer as you make other kinds of mobiles and experiment with them.

OTHER SYMMETRICAL MOBILES

Alexander Calder and other sculptors created mobiles with a variety of shapes suspended from the main balancing beam. Symmetrical mobiles can use shapes other than rectangles, as long as the total weight of the shapes on one side balances the total weight of those hanging on the other side.

You can modify the mobile you constructed in the previous activity in a number of ways. It is fun and interesting to see how one shape can be substituted for another and still keep the entire mobile balanced. This will give the mobile a different look and allow you to learn more about balancing.

You will need:

> the complete mobile from pages 75–77
> 3 or more pieces of cardboard, at least 12 inches wide and 24 inches long
> scissors
> masking tape

Challenges and Experiments to Try

The mobile from the previous activity has two identical sides. Remove all of the pieces hanging on one side. Try hanging different-shaped pieces of cardboard in their place.

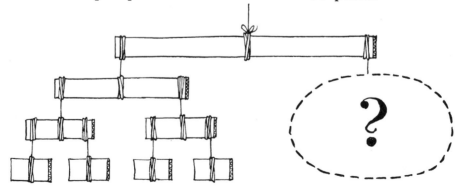

- Can you cut out a single piece of cardboard, rectangular in shape, that will balance the set of hanging pieces?
- Can you cut out a single piece of cardboard, triangular in shape, that will balance the set of hanging pieces?
- Can you cut out a single piece of cardboard, roughly oval in shape, that will balance the set of hanging pieces?

What's Happening?

Objects of equal weight on each side of the main beam will balance. In order to balance the mobile with a single piece of cardboard, you must replace the set of 7 pieces with a piece that is equal in weight. Assuming the piece of cardboard you will be using now is the same weight as the pieces of cardboard you used for the previous mobile, you must cut out a rectangle that is equal in area to all of the smaller pieces. Start with a big piece of cardboard and gradually cut off pieces until the remaining piece just about balances the other side of the mobile. The area of the big rectangle should be equal to the sum of all the areas of the smaller rectangles. (If you know how to find the area of a rectangle, you can use that formula to calculate what this sum is.)

Another approach is to line up all the pieces of cardboard that you took off the mobile and form them into a rectangle. Here is one way you can arrange the pieces.

12 INCHES			
6 INCHES		6 INCHES	
3 INCHES	3 INCHES	3 INCHES	3 INCHES

Make an outline of this rectangle on the large piece of cardboard. Cut out this shape. It should balance the other side of the mobile. If you rearrange the pieces, you will have a rectangle with different dimensions. This shape should also balance the set of pieces.

12 INCHES		3 INCHES	3 INCHES
6 INCHES	6 INCHES	3 INCHES	3 INCHES

You can also try forming a triangle from the smaller pieces, or by calculating an area of the triangle that is equal to the area of the set of pieces. Another approach is to cut the 6-by-12-inch rectangle in half diagonally. Then tape the pieces together to form a complete triangle.

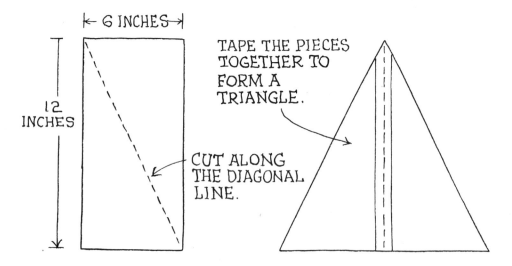

⊢ 6 INCHES ⊣

12 INCHES

TAPE THE PIECES TOGETHER TO FORM A TRIANGLE.

CUT ALONG THE DIAGONAL LINE.

Making an oval shape is more challenging. You can form a rough oval shape by lining up the pieces of cardboard as shown. Note that even though two 3-inch pieces are not used, their contribution is the area filled in around the other pieces to make an oval shape.

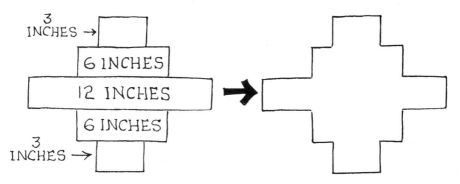

Using this same method, you can make a variety of different shapes that are equal in area to the set of hanging pieces. These new shapes will still keep the mobile in balance.

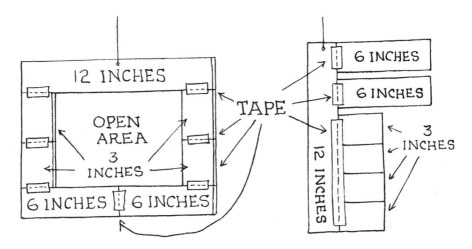

All of these substitute shapes show that as long as you replace the set of pieces with a shape that is equal in area to the set, the mobile will balance. However, remember that the big piece of cardboard you use has to be the same weight as the pieces of cardboard you used for your original mobile. If you try to replace the pieces of cardboard with shapes cut from other types of materials, such as wood or plastic, the mobile will no longer balance, even if these shapes are equal in area to the pieces of cardboard. This is because equal areas of different materials do not necessarily weigh the same.

A Further Challenge

Cut out 1-inch squares of cardboard. How many of these squares will be needed to balance a 6-inch square?

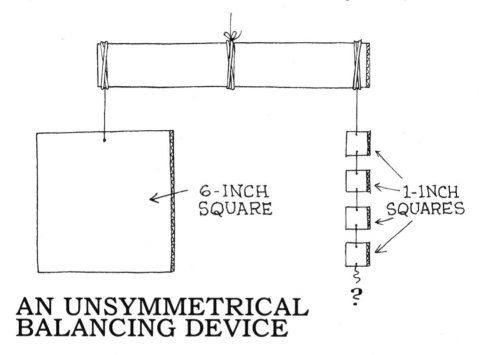

6-INCH SQUARE

1-1NCH SQUARES

?

AN UNSYMMETRICAL BALANCING DEVICE

In most circus balancing acts, there are usually an equal number of performers on each side of a balancing point. In some acts, this symmetry isn't present. One performer may be balancing several others at the opposite end of a long pole. This doesn't seem to fit with the previous investigations. How and why does this happen? The next activities will help you understand what has to be done to make it happen.

You will need:

      10 books or wooden blocks, all the same size
      10 pieces of cardboard, 2 inches wide and 24 inches
         long
      2 tables or desks

84

Challenges and Experiments to Try

An interesting challenge is to see how far from the edge of a table you can extend a stack of books or blocks.

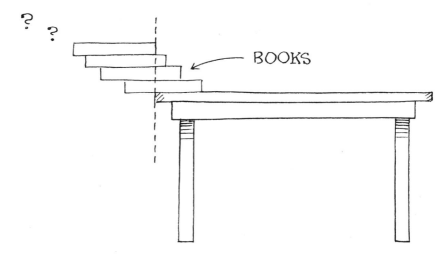

BOOKS

- Now try stacking the pieces of cardboard. How far out from the edge of the table can you stack 10 pieces of cardboard without their tipping over? (The cardboard on the table cannot be taped to it.)

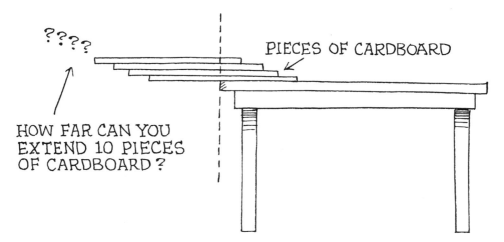

PIECES OF CARDBOARD

HOW FAR CAN YOU EXTEND 10 PIECES OF CARDBOARD?

- How far can you stack 2, 3, 4, or 5 pieces of cardboard without their falling off the table?

- Now stack the pieces of cardboard on top of one another so that each new piece extends farther from the edge of the table until the entire top piece is just over the edge of the table. What is the least number of pieces of cardboard you can stack on top of one another to achieve this position?

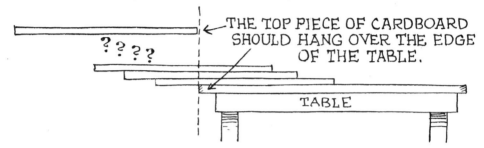

? ? ? ?

THE TOP PIECE OF CARDBOARD SHOULD HANG OVER THE EDGE OF THE TABLE.

TABLE

- Try different stacking patterns to achieve the same position for the top piece. How does the number of pieces of cardboard you use with each compare to the number you used in the last experiment?
- Collect 10 books of the same size and try stacking them.
- What is the minimum number of books, blocks, or pieces of cardboard you must use to form a bridge spanning two tables or desks several feet apart? (Hint: You may have to cut more pieces of cardboard.)

What's Happening?

If a piece of cardboard extends beyond the edge of the table, it will remain balanced as long as its midpoint does not extend beyond the table edge. The half extending over the edge has to be counterbalanced by the half that is resting on the table.

When you try to balance 2 pieces of cardboard, more than half of the bottom piece must rest on the table. The top piece can have its midpoint located beyond the edge of the table. The bottom piece has to counterbalance the portion of itself that extends beyond the table as well as the portion of the second piece that extends beyond the table.

As you add more and more pieces of cardboard, the midpoint of the top piece extends farther beyond the edge of the table. The bottom pieces have to be moved in the opposite direction in order to counterbalance this hanging weight. If you are very careful in your adjustment of each piece, it is possible to have the 10 pieces extend 2 feet or more from the table.

This distance will vary depending on the thickness of the cardboard you are using. The thicker the cardboard, the more pieces you will need in order to have the top one extend over the edge of the table. Likewise, you will need a greater number of books compared to cardboard pieces for the top one to extend over the edge of the table.

When you experimented with alternate ways of stacking, did you come up with any that allowed you to use fewer pieces of cardboard? You should have found that you need to stack only 6 or even 5 pieces of cardboard in order to get the top piece to extend over the edge of the table when the pieces are stacked this way.

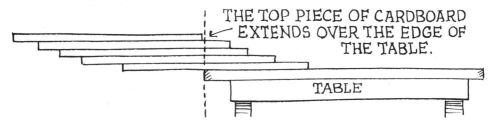

THE TOP PIECE OF CARDBOARD EXTENDS OVER THE EDGE OF THE TABLE.

TABLE

And you may have needed even fewer pieces of cardboard if you used this pattern.

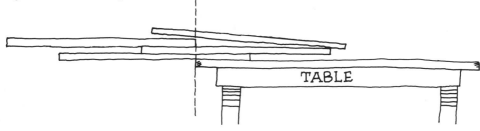

TABLE

Alternative ways of stacking may allow you to use even fewer pieces to accomplish the same result.

You can construct a bridge with the pieces of cardboard, employing the same approach you used for a single extension. However, here you have to put a piece of cardboard in the middle on top of the two extensions to make the bridge, and this middle piece is away from the edges of both tables. Therefore, you have to add more pieces of cardboard to the tabletop stacks on both sides of your bridge to counterbalance the weight of the pieces that are away from the table.

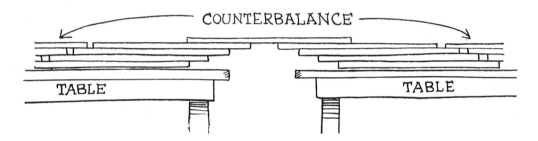

The way you stacked the pieces of cardboard is similar to the way the ancient Roman engineers built some bridges and parts of buildings. Specially cut blocks were stacked to support a balanced extension. Another extension came from the opposite direction. Together they resulted in a bridgelike structure called a *corbel*.

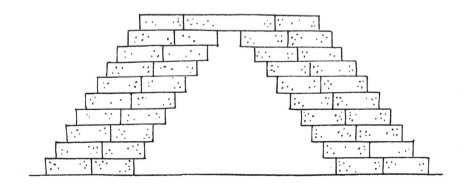

A modern-day suspension bridge can be thought of as a gigantic balancing act. The towers and cables at each end of the bridge help anchor and support the highway platform that extends beyond the towers.

Each tower helps support the highway platform. It also helps transfer some of the weight of the platform to the shore. The cables are pulled down by the weight of the platform. Some of this weight is transferred to the tower, and some of it is transferred to the shore.

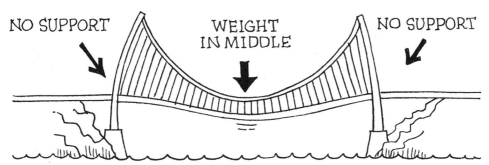

NO SUPPORT   WEIGHT IN MIDDLE   NO SUPPORT

THERE IS NO SUPPORT AT EITHER END AND THE TOWERS BEND UNDER THE WEIGHT OF THE HIGHWAY PLATFORM.

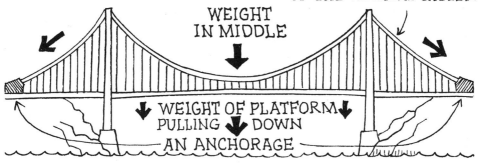

THE CABLES KEEP THE TOWER UPRIGHT AND BALANCE THE PULL OF THE VERTICAL CABLES.

WEIGHT IN MIDDLE

WEIGHT OF PLATFORM PULLING DOWN

AN ANCHORAGE

THE WEIGHT OF THE HIGHWAY PLATFORM IS BALANCED BY THE TOWERS AND THE CABLES.

AN UNSYMMETRICAL MOBILE

What do you think might happen if you turned your stacking arrangement upside down and made it into a mobile? You'll find out in this section!

As you experiment with the next mobile, observe how it is like or unlike the previous balancing structures you have made.

You will need:

      the pieces of cardboard from page 84
      10 to 20 nails, 2 inches long
      rubber bands
      thin string
      scissors

Step 1. Wrap a rubber band securely around the middle of a piece of cardboard. Tie a 6-inch piece of string to the rubber band. Adjust the rubber band so that cardboard piece A balances horizontally when you hold it up by the string.

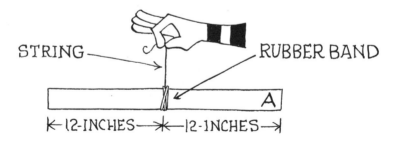

Step 2. Place 2 rubber bands on another piece of cardboard, B, as shown in the drawing. Make sure they are wrapped tightly. Tie a 6-inch piece of string to the rubber band farther from the end.

TIE THE STRING TO
THIS RUBBER BAND.

B

Step 3. Tie the string from cardboard A to the rubber band on the end of cardboard B. Move the other rubber band on cardboard B so that cardboard B balances horizontally.

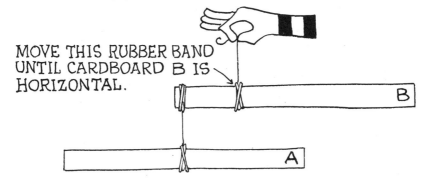

MOVE THIS RUBBER BAND
UNTIL CARDBOARD B IS
HORIZONTAL.

B

A

Step 4. Repeat the same steps to attach a third piece of cardboard. Attach cardboard C to cardboards B and A, as shown in the drawing. Adjust cardboard C so that it balances horizontally.

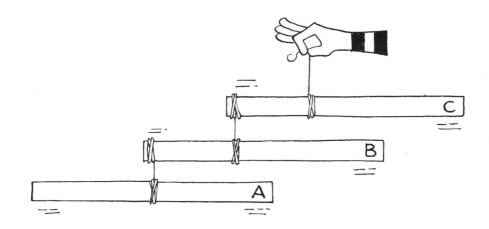

C

B

A

Step 5. Keep adding pieces of cardboard until the end of the top piece hangs beyond the end of the bottom piece as shown. How many pieces of cardboard do you have to attach before this happens?

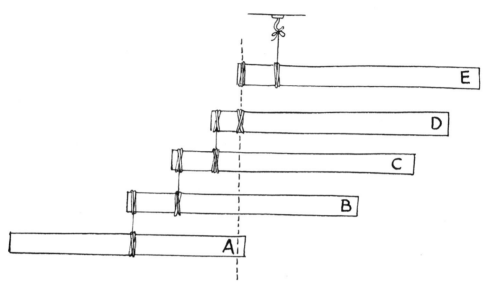

Challenges and Experiments to Try

When you assembled your mobile, you had to rebalance the top piece each time you added a piece. The pieces below should have remained balanced. As you perform the following experiments, try to predict what will happen when you change the positions of the rubber bands.

- Start with the bottom piece, cardboard A. What happens if the rubber band is moved about 2 inches in either direction? Does this affect the balance of the other pieces?

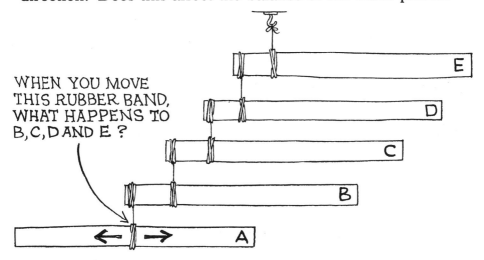

WHEN YOU MOVE
THIS RUBBER BAND,
WHAT HAPPENS TO
B, C, D AND E ?

- What happens if the rubber band closer to the center on cardboard B is moved about 2 inches in either direction? Does this affect the balance of the pieces above or below?

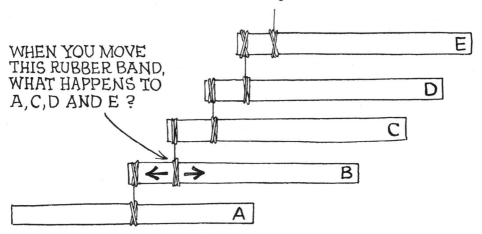

WHEN YOU MOVE
THIS RUBBER BAND,
WHAT HAPPENS TO
A, C, D AND E ?

- Do the same thing for cardboards C, D, and E. Can you predict how changing the balance of each piece of cardboard will affect the balance of the other pieces?

- You can try another set of experiments on this mobile, too. What do you think will happen if a weight is added to one of the pieces?
- Wrap 10 nails together with a rubber band and attach them to either end of cardboard A with another rubber band. Try to predict what will happen to all the other pieces of cardboard when this weight is added.

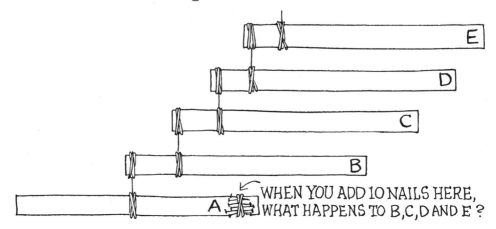

WHEN YOU ADD 10 NAILS HERE, WHAT HAPPENS TO B,C,D AND E ?

- Add the bunch of nails to each of the other pieces of cardboard in turn and see what happens.

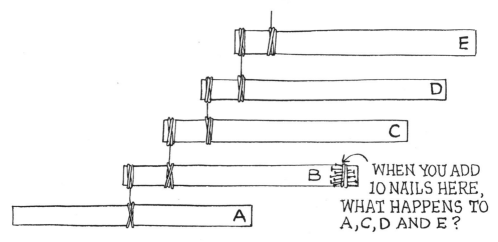

WHEN YOU ADD 10 NAILS HERE, WHAT HAPPENS TO A,C,D AND E ?

- Make up other experiments in which you add a different number of nails to different pieces of cardboard.

What's Happening?

This mobile looks very different from the symmetrical one. The arrangement is unsymmetrical because the balancing point is different on each succeeding level. Also, except for the bottom piece, the balancing point of each piece of cardboard is away from the midpoint.

As you add more pieces of cardboard, the topmost piece has to support more weight on one end compared to the other pieces. To compensate for this added weight, the balancing point is moved closer to the end where the extra weight is hanging. The part of the piece opposite this end counter-balances this weight. If you were to keep the balancing point at the midpoint, you would have to add extra weight at the end opposite from where all the other pieces of cardboard hang.

When you move the center rubber band on each piece of cardboard, you should find that the balance of only that piece is affected. The pieces above and below remain balanced because you haven't changed the weight of any of these pieces. But moving the rubber band does change the balance of the piece of cardboard it is attached to, because more weight is now on one side of the balancing point than on the other.

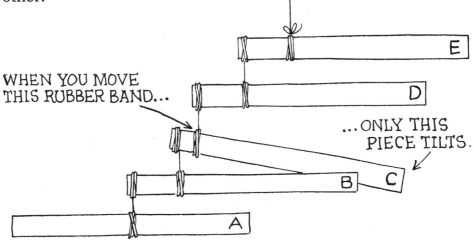

WHEN YOU MOVE THIS RUBBER BAND...

...ONLY THIS PIECE TILTS.

Adding nails to one of the pieces of cardboard does have a noticeable effect on that piece and the ones above it. However, the pieces below are not affected. The pieces above support all the weight of those below, so adding nails to any piece will change the balance of the pieces above it.

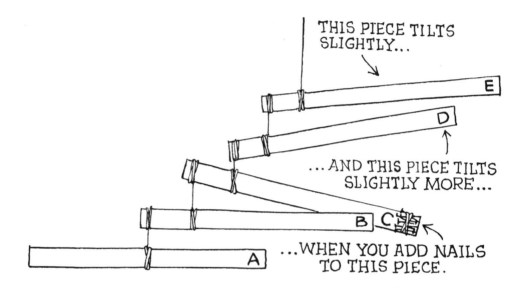

As you go up the set of mobile pieces, the balancing point moves closer and closer to one end. Therefore, the position of the pieces near the top will be less changed if a weight is added to the edge of the short end. On the other hand, adding a weight to the long end, especially on the top pieces, will have a big effect. These ends will hang almost vertically.

Further Challenges

You can change your unsymmetrical mobile in a number of ways to produce other interesting arrangements and movements. Here are some different arrangements that you can make with your mobile. Try moving the rubber bands or adding nails to achieve the same results.

96

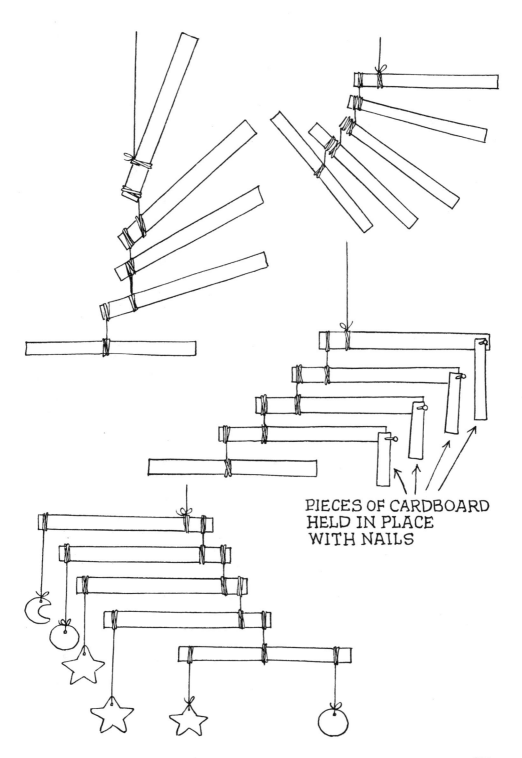

PIECES OF CARDBOARD
HELD IN PLACE
WITH NAILS

A SIMPLE BALANCE

When scientists investigate something, they look for the characteristics that certain examples or situations have in common. Then they often build models that include all these characteristics. Some of your constructions, such as the pieces of cardboard that represent circus performers, are models of real situations. Your models help you understand the real situation because you can control what happens easily and make changes quickly.

Throughout your explorations, you saw that the amount of weight placed on one side of a balancing object had to be balanced by an equal amount of weight on the opposite side of the balancing point. You also discovered that where the weight was positioned determined whether or not an object would balance.

These observations can be explored further by building a

device called a *simple balance*. A simple balance is a beam that has its balancing point in the middle and a pan at each end for adding weight. If you build and use it carefully, the simple balance makes it possible for you to calculate and predict regular patterns of balancing weights. These relationships are so exact that you can devise mathematical formulas for them.

Although today most balances are electronic and some are quite complicated and expensive, a piece of cardboard or wood balanced on a coat-hanger wire can work almost as well.

You will need:

> 2 pieces of cardboard, 2 inches wide and 20 inches long
>
> 1 pound of nails, 2½ inches long
>
> 10 big paper clips
>
> masking tape
>
> 1 piece of coat-hanger wire or any sturdy wire, at least 8 inches long
>
> ruler
>
> scissors
>
> rubber bands
>
> pencil
>
> paper
>
> table

Step 1. Draw a line down the middle of a piece of cardboard. Score, or cut slightly, along this line partway into the cardboard. Be careful not to cut through to the other side.

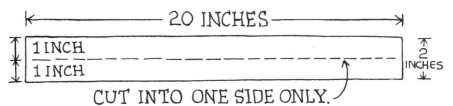

Step 2. Tape the other piece of cardboard upright in front of the scored line on the bottom piece. Fold up the half of the scored piece behind the upright piece as shown in the drawing. Tape it to the upright piece.

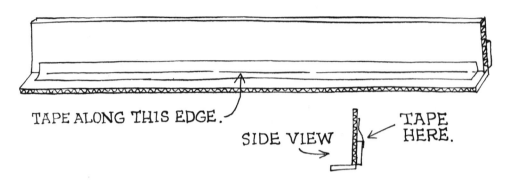

TAPE ALONG THIS EDGE.

SIDE VIEW

TAPE HERE.

Step 3. Starting from the center of the cardboard, make a mark every inch along the bottom piece. Do this on both sides of the center.

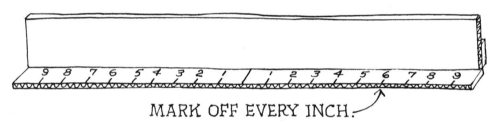

MARK OFF EVERY INCH.

Step 4. Place masking tape on the pieces of cardboard so that the bottom piece is at a right angle to the upright piece.

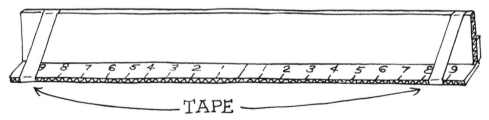

TAPE

Step 5. Find the midpoint on the upright section of cardboard and make a mark about ¼ inch from the top. Push a coat-hanger wire all the way through the midpoint of the cardboard. Check to see that the piece of cardboard can swing easily on the wire.

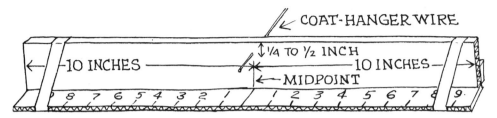

Step 6. Tape an end of the coat-hanger wire to the edge of a table. Allow enough room for the cardboard balance arm to swing freely without falling off the wire.

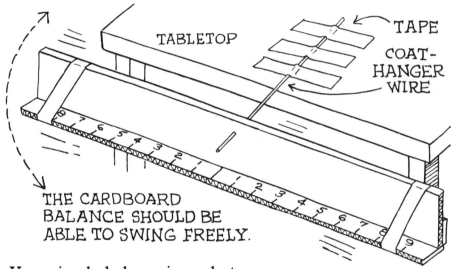

Your simple balance is ready to use.

Challenges and Experiments to Try

To perform these experiments, you can insert nails into the exposed holes of the bottom piece of cardboard. The number and location of the nails will determine whether or not the beam will balance horizontally. Try the following arrangements and then make up your own combinations. Record your results and look for patterns.

- What happens when you insert a nail at a time into each inch mark from 1 to 9? How does the position of the balance beam change as you move farther away from the midpoint?
- You can join nails together with rubber bands and insert them into the holes. What happens to the balance beam as you add more and more nails to a position?
- Place 10 nails at the 5-inch position on one side of the balance beam. How many different ways can you balance this set of nails?
- Place 2 nails at the 4-inch position on one side of the balance beam. Where do you have to place 1 nail on the other side of the midpoint to balance the beam?

What's Happening?

The results you obtained with the simple balance should by now seem familiar to you. The farther from the balancing point you place a weight, the more unbalanced the beam becomes. As you add more and more nails to a point on the balance beam, you make it tilt more.

As you try different combinations on the right and left sides of the balance beam, you may have noticed some patterns and relationships. For example, placing 2 nails at the 4-inch mark will balance 1 nail at the 8-inch mark.

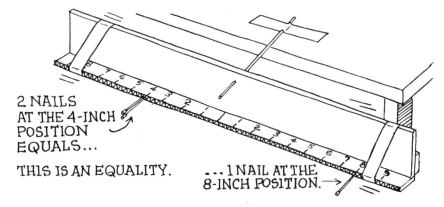

2 NAILS AT THE 4-INCH POSITION EQUALS...

THIS IS AN EQUALITY.

...1 NAIL AT THE 8-INCH POSITION. →

This relationship can also be expressed as a mathematical equation: $2 \times 4 = 8 = 1 \times 8$.

Putting 3 nails at the 2-inch mark will balance 2 nails at the 3-inch mark: $3 \times 2 = 6 = 2 \times 3$.

These equations can be expressed in an abstract mathematical way. The product of the weight on one side multiplied by its distance from the midpoint is equal to the product of the weight on the opposite side multiplied by its distance from the midpoint. The relationship is expressed in this mathematical formula: $w_1 \times d_1 = w_2 \times d_2$.

This simple formula is the basis of calculations for the design of structures from bridges to skyscrapers.

EXPLORING BALANCES

Use your imagination to create even more mobiles and balancing toys. You can assemble simple shapes and objects made of cardboard, wood, metal, and plastic and follow the techniques you've learned here.

Ideas for new constructions are all around you. Take a walk and look at buildings, bridges, and playground equipment. At the library, you can find books about the sculptures of Alexander Calder. Look at pictures of acrobats or maybe even watch some exciting balancing acts in person if a circus comes to your town. Can you invent your own designs based on these real situations?

As you build your own models, try to make arrangements that balance in the same way as real-life structures.